To Trish & John
Simon & Emma

With love

Carol

Aug. 1993

WIDER HORIZONS

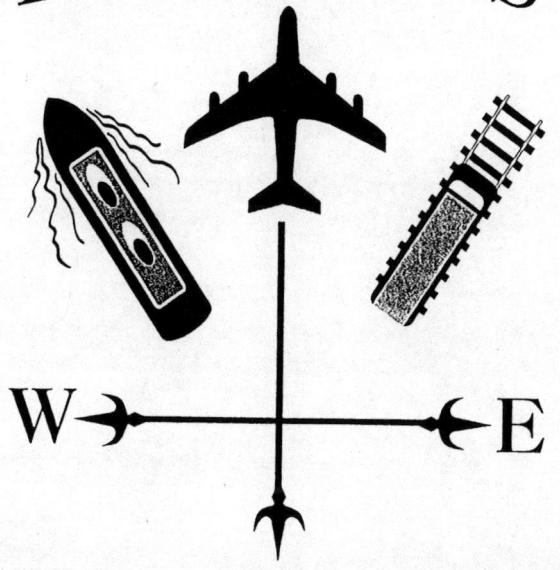

W   E

WIDER
HORIZONS

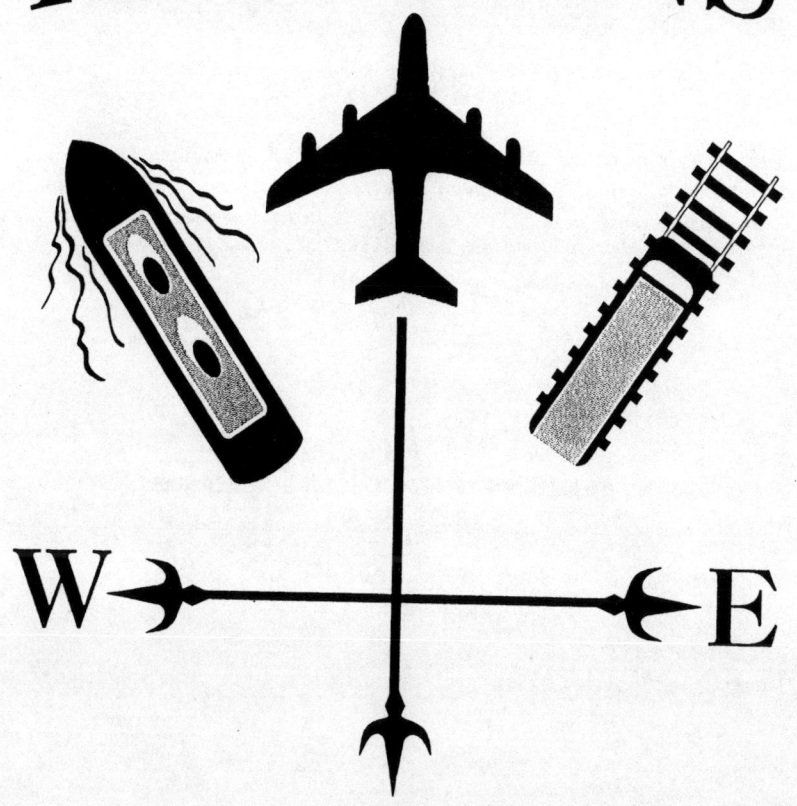

W   E

Carol Stephens

Published in 1993 by
Carol Stephens

British Library Cataloguing in Publication Data
A catalogue record for this book is available from the British Library

ISBN 0 9520850 0 3

Designed and Produced by Images Design and Print Ltd
Printed and Bound in Great Britain

To Henry

Drawing by our Grandson Sam

Thanks to Kathy Davies for her
help and advice

PORTUGAL 1969

This was our very first trip abroad together. It was a business trip taken just before Henry's retirement and unfortunately I did not keep a diary, so have to rely on memory and outstanding impressions. I was terrified of flying having lost a beloved brother, Charles, in an air crash in 1955, and I distinctly remember gripping Henry's hand during take-off and landing. How blasé I have become!

We flew to Lisbon, a beautiful city with wide avenues and intriguing shops. A customer sent a car to collect us from our hotel, and we visited his carpet factory in an old convent in Estramose, where we saw girls doing most intricate work on looms. The owner spoke very little English, and we no Portuguese, so conversation was very limited. He put a car at our disposal together with a driver named Antonio. His English too, was limited, but he was a great soccer fan and spoke of "Football" and knew the names of all our players. With the aid of many gestures and a dictionary we got along famously, and he took us to local beauty spots, and, at our wish, to a ceramic and pottery dealer. I found the ware most attractive, and purchased a water bottle similar to one I had noticed in a cool corner at the carpet factory. I would have liked to have had more, but one is so limited when flying.

We went to Portalegre to visit another customer, and when business was done we hired a car and set off on our own to explore. We made our way first to the Algarve, of which we had heard so much. There were lovely beaches rather spoilt by the backdrop of huge concrete buildings being built to house thousands of tourists.

The country was most beautiful inland and up in the mountains, and the people warm and welcoming. We stayed in Pousadas, which are often old castles or monasteries run by the government. I recall waking Henry in the early hours to join me on the balcony to listen to a Nightingale singing his heart out. We met many herds of goats with tinkling bells hung around their necks, often being driven to new pastures by very young boys.

En route to Cape Town

We made our way to Lisbon where we had arranged to meet our friends Maurice and Morna, who were cruising on a luxurious Cunard liner. This was one of their ports of call so we brought them ashore and drove them to Cascais, where the very wealthy have beautiful houses. Here we enjoyed a meal in the open air and my first taste of Vinho Verde. After seeing them back on board we made our way north to Cape St Vincent, a wild rocky area of heather and lichen and scrub. Here it was that Henry the Navigator gathered together his Astrologers, Shipbuilders and Geographers in the fort, which still stands, and where he planned his voyages. The fort now houses a museum where we saw a film of Henry's life and discoveries.

Our visit was only about ten days, but I was most impressed with the country, and hope very much, to visit it again.

—————————————— ⳩ ——————————————

SOUTH AFRICA
VOYAGE TO CAPE TOWN

We left Island House in 1970 after twenty-one happy years, put the furniture in store, and took up temporary residence in our holiday house in Pembrokeshire, and it was from here that we set off on our travels to South Africa. It seemed very strange, shutting the door of our little semi-detached house to undertake such a tremendous journey.

We planned to collect Jonathan in Cardiff, he would then take over our car and drive us to Southampton. We stopped in Swansea to do some last minute shopping, and Henry got lost when he went to find a toilet, and I was left in the car park for what seemed ages – a fine start to our trip!

We stayed a night in Porthcawl and celebrated the start of our holiday by eating and drinking too much, then spent the rest of the evening in our room sorting out papers and labelling luggage. Ellinor was very much in our thoughts as she was off to Norway soon to take up her first appointment as a qualified Physiotherapist in a strange country with no knowledge of the language.

Having collected Jonathan the three of us spent a night in Southampton, and in the morning assembled our luggage and made for the docks where a Cook's representative took charge and escorted us aboard the SS *Vaal*, our home for the next twelve days. Our cabin looked quite cosy and we were delighted to find a telegram from Jonathan, Hugh and Ellinor wishing us *Bon Voyage* together with a box of lovely spring flowers which gave a great deal of pleasure for some time.

We all had a drink together in the Orangery then it was time for Jonathan to go ashore. There were streamers everywhere, from boat to dock, a great deal of excitement and noise with people all waving and cheering and shouting last minute messages. The Pilot left the boat at 2.45 and we passed The Needles at 3 o'clock, and it was then that we felt we had really and truly started on our adventures.

Back in our cabin our steward introduced himself; he was a Scot with a strong Glaswegian accent, which I had difficulty in understanding at times.

It was hard to imagine we were moving at all, the ship was so steady, but in the night a heavy rolling motion woke me as we entered the Bay of Biscay, and next morning I breakfasted alone as Henry was not feeling too good. I managed a walk on the promenade deck despite the roll and high seas.

We were seated at a table in the saloon in the Commodore's Compound in the company of a retired Squadron Leader, Jim Adams and his daughter Gill - who had just left school - who were going to live outside Johannesburg. He had known my brother Charles in the RAF.

A warning came over the tannoy telling us to make sure everything in our cabin was fixed firmly as the Captain was about to do a quick turnabout in answer to an SOS thirty-six miles away. This was at 2 p.m. and we expected to reach the incident at 3 p.m. with the wind at 41 knots. However, another ship got there first, so we about-turned again amid terrific seas, with glasses sliding off tables and the promenade deck awash. Once on course again and past Finisterre, all became calmer, thank goodness, and I am pleased to say Henry recovered sufficiently to attend the Captain's cocktail party, which was not very exciting and must be rather boring for the Captain and his lady.

Williams, our steward, woke us up with a cup of tea next day with a cheery "Good morning, it's a lovely day the noo" and after breakfast we entered into the ship's activities, first of all by attending Divine service on deck enjoying the hymn singing tremendously – then playing Shuffleboard for the first time. We chose The Cellar for our aperitifs and met a retired bank manager and his wife, and a builder and his wife from Coventry, who were all good fun and with whom we met up again after dinner. We retired to our bunks a little the worse for wear.

Next day we sighted land and watched it take the shape of mountains and then buildings as the port of Las Palmas appeared. It was fascinating to watch the busy little tugs pushing and pulling until we were docked alongside the jetty between a Russian ship and a Portuguese vessel. Quite a few passengers disembarked permanently, and we went ashore after an early lunch and shared a taxi with fellow passengers to the town. The driver did not speak English and gestured wildly with both hands which we found extremely alarming, but we managed to make him understand that we wished to be dropped at the Cathedral. Unfortunately it was siesta time, with all the shops closed and even the priests having a nap, and we went our separate ways to explore the town. It was not very interesting, rather dirty and smelly, but we enjoyed nosing around on terra firma and eventually took a taxi back to the ship for a welcome cup of tea. We had, apparently, called for refuelling and were now being manoeuvred by the tugs into the open sea.

It would be too boring to relate our day to day activities, suffice to say we entered into the fun on board and got to know our fellow travellers better. The Surgeon/Commander knew Chris Hudson, our niece's husband, who was, apparently, renowned for wearing a bowler hat when attending lectures. The temperature rose noticeably and we enjoyed the swimming pool when it was not too crowded.

From the weather reports we gathered that the U.K was having a bad time with snow and blizzards, which was hard to imagine when we were only a week away with the temperature in the 80's. We did experience a violent thunderstorm one day when the chairs had to be moved to the starboard side under cover, and the pool had to be emptied. We joined a small party for a tour of the Bridge, conducted by a 2nd Officer in the Middle Watch, which was very interesting.

The storm passed and the sea looked a deep indigo as we entered a busy shipping lane and encountered a variety of vessels. In the cinema whilst watching some absurd film, I could not help thinking how strange it all was, feeling the throb of the engines, six hours from the Equator with nothing but water to see in all directions and goodness knows what depth below us. Next day we witnessed the "Crossing the Line" ceremony when "King Neptune" appeared draped in a lot of seaweed and very little else, and initiated five victims by ducking them in the pool.

Dolphins and flying fish were now a common sight. Gala night arrived and many people were in fancy dress. We had to collect our own supper of fish and chips served in paper from the galley, and a message came over the Tannoy at about 0100 saying, "Will the parents occupying cabin number – please go and attend their offspring who is busy gnawing its way through the bulkhead." So life on board continued and being quite a new experience for us we enjoyed it all, but we both agreed a cruise would not be our choice for a holiday.

The sea became rougher and the wind stronger as we approached South Africa with the temperature in the 80's. It was too rough to swim, indeed the pool had to be emptied again, and our last night on board was very rough indeed.

Henry slept through it all, but I had to phone the Bridge to report a rattle in the bulkhead which was driving me mad. I was sick next day whilst coping with our last bit of packing, but recovered quite quickly once I was on deck in the fresh air.

Williams had told us it was well worth rising early to see Cape Town at dawn, and this we did on Wednesday March 11th at 6 a.m. There was a deep red sky over the Hottentot range on the port side, and the buildings of Cape Town gradually took shape with the famous Table Mountain in the background on our starboard. As we watched the tug busily nosing us into harbour, the sun, now a huge orange sphere, rose and gradually lit up the view before us. It was an unforgettable sight.

We said farewell to our shipboard friends, cleared customs and immigration, and, stepping onto South African soil, were delighted to find Jessie and Frank, Henry's cousin and his wife, who were to be our hosts for a while, on the dock to welcome us.

SOUTH AFRICA
CAPE TOWN

There was a great welcome awaiting us at Mulvihal Road, Rondebosch, where we met Jessie's mother, Mrs Teagle, known as Gran and a wonderful lady of 90; Lizzie, a large Bantu servant with a smile to match, and Impi (Zulu for Warrior) the black Labrador. Robert, their son, who had recently completed his National Service, and is now employed by the Nederland Bank, is a delightful young man, with, I imagine, a great future before him. He appeared later with his girl friend, Helen. We got to know the couple well as they visited us on several occasions in the U.K after their marriage.

From our bedroom window we had a wonderful view of Table Mountain, which was clear that day, but often the summit was covered in mist known as the table-cloth. After lunch we were driven to the nearest beach – Milnerton – and walked with bare feet on the whitest sand I have ever seen. I was stung by a bluebottle Jelly fish, a strange creature with wings and a long thread of a tail which holds the sting. Later, after sunset, we went up the 1250 ft high Signal Hill where we had a wonderful view of Cape Town and our ship SS *Vaal* in the harbour, illuminated with a myriad lights. On our right was a tiny green light ascending Table Mountain, which was the cable car.

This wonderful city was founded by Van Reibeeck in 1652 as a victualing station for the ships of the Dutch East Indies Company on their way to and from the East.

It was good to feel everything steady beneath our feet on our first night ashore. We slept well and were awakened by

21

Lizzie bearing tea and wearing a huge smile. Gran always had her breakfast in bed and I made a habit of having a chat with her at this time. She was a remarkable character. She had left a small town in Somerset to join and wed her fiance, a mining engineer, and settled in Lusaka where she was the only white woman, her nearest white neighbours being missionaries twenty miles away. She lost her first child and brought up Jessie and her brother John until they were old enough to complete their education in England. Frank and Jessie met on board a liner when Jess was returning home from England. Frank was travelling to the Cape to take up an appointment with the Royal Insurance Company, in whose employment he remained for thirty-five years, and retired in 1969 as representative for the whole of Cape Province.

They gave us a wonderful time. We visited museums, one being Groot Constantia, the first wine producing farm, now two hundred and fifty years old and still producing good wines. The building itself was Dutch architecture, which I found very attractive. We met some very interesting people. One day attending a luncheon at the City Club, of which Frank was a member, I sat next to the guest speaker, a Mr. Van den Vat, the representative of *The Times* in South Africa. Both he and his wife graduated from Durham University having read Classics.

We attended a re-union lunch at British Nylon Spinners S.A given in our honour, and it was fun meeting people we had known in Pontypool. Later we drove to Chapman's Peak and Hout Bay to the south of the city, passing beneath mountains known as the Twelve Apostles, and along the coast up to Sentinel Peak where we stood looking across the Atlantic.

We dined at the Kelvin Club, a Country Club which has everything including golf, swimming and horse riding. It was a beautiful house once the residence of a wealthy Dutch merchant and stood in immaculate gardens.

We went to the races at Kensington, where we were invited by the Steward of the Jockey Club to lunch. Frank was a stickler for protocol and we had to pass muster, hats and gloves being the order of the day. I wore a white suit and borrowed white gloves from Gran, and a white scarf to adorn a yellow hat which I had purchased on board. At lunch I sat next to a Minister of the Government, and opposite poor Frank who was perspiring with anxiety. One of the first pieces of advice he gave us, was never to discuss politics! My neighbour was rather naughty, questioning me a lot, but I pleaded ignorance on most subjects, he must have thought me very stupid!

A day at the races

Henry and I spent a day in the city on our own, visiting the Rhodes statue in the grounds of the University, which we though an atrocity. We went on to the Castle, the oldest building in Cape Town dated 1666 and kept in an excellent state of preservation. This building was originally right on the shore, but now stands well inland as so much land has been reclaimed.

23

Taking lunch at a restaurant, I remember feeling improperly dressed as everyone dresses impeccably for the city. It was our intention to go up Table Mountain, and we watched weather conditions anxiously, as a mist was hanging on the summit, but on emerging from the Cafe Royal it was glorious, and we took the cable car to the top, which was a bit hair-raising. The view was magnificent, and when walking along the rocky surface in glorious sunshine, one felt on top of the world. We had to take two buses and a train to reach home, and arrived hot and dusty, but recovered after a shower and a change. Frank's daughter Trish and her husband John, joined us for a meal. They lived at the top of a block of flats in Milnerton with a lovely view of the mountains. We knew Trish, of course as she had stayed with us in the U.K, but we had not met John before. They were expecting their first child in two month's time.

Every Saturday, Frank and Jess went shopping in the market very early, and were back for breakfast at 8 o'clock. We often went for a walk following a track half way up the Table Mountain, through pine forest which kept us comparatively cool in the heat of the day, with the warmth of the sun bringing out a strong smell of the pines.

We paid another visit to the races and stood in the Turf member's enclosure, not a profitable visit but I got as much pleasure from watching the expensively dressed people as I did from the racing. The Coloureds and the Natives had their separate enclosure, but this has probably changed now.

We planned a trip in Frank's car to start after the Easter holidays, to give the children time to return to their studies. This was the first holiday Frank and Jess had taken since his retirement and there was a great deal of excitement and planning, with maps spread over the floor and Jess and I cooking for picnics. There was no Lizzie to help as she was spending a night at her chapel singing and praying.

A client of Frank's had asked him to get tickets for the Easter races, and Henry and I went with him to deliver them. We drove to the Wynberg area of Cape Town, to a delightful old farmhouse standing in one hundred and twenty five acres, many of them growing vines. There we met the owner, Strip Mennel, a millionaire from Johannesburg; the owner of several gold mines. This was his country retreat and he was alone as his wife had left for a visit to their family in England. He was to follow when the last of the grapes had been harvested. He was a delightful and very interesting man who had left London at the age of seventeen to seek his fortune in South Africa, and I wish I had heard his full story. He had even explored the sea for diamonds, and sold out to De Beers, and I recall this theme was introduced into one of Wilbur Smith's books.

He invited us to go down a mine when we were in Johannesberg, but on consulting our itinerary, we found we would be there on a Saturday and Sunday when the mines were closed. He insisted however, that Frank got in touch with his Secretary to arrange for tickets to the Gold Mine dances to be sent to us at our hotel.

He told us that workers from so many different tribes were employed, that the only way to instruct them was by graphic display on blackboard. They were probably used to using tools such as spades and picks, but they were not familiar with knives and forks, or even a toilet. Many of these tribes were antagonistic to each other, and to avoid fighting they were encouraged to compete in the dances every Sunday.

We were very sad to read a report in the papers on our return home, that Strip Mennel had died of a heart attack during his voyage to the U.K.

Before our holiday, we took Gran for a drive through the wine growing area of Stellenbosch, home of the Afrikaans

University. The drive took us through the Hellschoogte Pass, wonderful mountain territory, to Franschhoek, where we visited the Huguenot museum and memorial which had been carefully reconstructed using original material from Saaveld, the mansion in Cape Town designed by Thibault in 1791. This was a drive of one hundred and ten miles in all, and Gran was as fresh as a daisy and enjoyed it all immensely.

SOUTH AFRICA
CAPE PROVINCE

We set off on Tuesday March 31st, planning to make the town of George our first stop. Frank drove for about one hundred and twenty miles going through the Du Toit Pass with its magnificent mountain scenery, the highest point being 2690 ft. The roads were superb and we gradually lost height and entered rolling plains similar to Salisbury plain, but on a vaster scale. We had a picnic lunch outside Heidelberg, and tea at Mossel Bay, passing through rather uninteresting country latterly, and arrived at Hawthorne Dene in George. We had travelled about one hundred and eighty miles and welcomed the comforts offered. I never ceased to be amazed at the amount of food Frank consumed. For breakfast he must have his porridge, followed by bacon and egg, sometimes kipper as well. He insisted on stopping for elevenses, then lunch, afternoon tea and an evening meal of three – four courses, and he doesn't look overweight, but am sure I will be after this run.

We had met friends of Frank and Jess's who were on their way to the Cape from Rhodesia, and Jess's brother John and his wife who happened to be camping in the woods. Frank seemed to have friends and acquaintances wherever we went.

We purchased a plentiful supply of canned of beer – this is thirsty work – and some meat pies, and entered the Outenigne Pass. The road followed a single track railway most of the way, and dropped down into lush valleys, then over rolling plains for miles and miles with the road fenced all the way to Oudsthoorn. We stopped to visit the Ostrich farm called Highgate, so named by the founder Will Hooper, who had been born in Highgate London. Here we waited for the guide in the shade of a huge Pepper tree. He was a tall handsome Adonis who wore Ostrich feathers in his trekkers hat. The tour lasted about two hours which culminated in a race between natives riding Ostriches! The farm covered five hundred morgens and housed some one thousand birds, the oldest known as Jack the Ripper, being aged forty-one years. The boys trapped a bird whilst Mike, our guide, explained its anatomy. For those who are interested, the Ostrich has fifteen vertebrae in its neck, has arm and hand joints, and is the only two-clawed bird. It is able to swallow a bottle the gullet being so large, and has enough brain to fill a dessertspoon. It swallows stones to help to grind food as it has no teeth, and has a vicious kick, so keep your distance! Its stomach has been found to contain 3lbs of small stones all worn round and smooth. One bird had a great liking for coins, and sadly died of copper poisoning.

At the ostrich farm

We were given a welcome cup of tea, and visited the shop. Mike draped a fantastic cape of superb feathers around my shoulders and I felt and looked liked Mae West. We purchased a few souvenirs, Henry having a spectacle case which lasted to the end of his days. It was so hot and dry as we had tea, that we could follow the course of a vehicle driving over the plains in the distance, by the cloud of dust which hung in the air over its trail.

We spent another night in George, then made for Port Elizabeth, passing through the heart of the famous Garden route before calling at Knysna, a delightful seaside resort with an inner lagoon. Once there we had coffee at The Heads, the opening to the Indian Ocean, then on to Plattenberg Bay, where we called on friends, Jack and Margaret Case – he being a retired Judge – and both made us very welcome. Their home consisted of several Rondaavels, each serving its own function one being in the library, one the lounge, one the kitchen etc – all situated in woodland, and aptly named, "The Sanctuary".

We found a solitary Inn in the wilds, The Heidof, a log cabin with furniture built entirely of solid wood, and here we had sandwiches. I imagine it would be a lovely holiday centre with many tempting walks. Our road went through mountainous country through two passes, the GrooteRiver Pass and the Blankrantz, with deep gorges on one side and dense woods on the other. Passing a noisy troop of baboons, we dropped down into Port Elizabeth, the third largest port, and the fifth largest city in South Africa.

There was a great deal of industry here, but it retained an English character as a result of the British settlers (this region is known as Settler country) who made their home here in 1820. We went for a short walk along the promenade after dinner, which reminded me very much of Blackpool. Incidentally, this was the first walk we had taken after dark.

Next day we visited the dolphinarium where we saw dolphins performing, the first time I had ever seen them. I do not care to see performing animals, but these creatures gave the impression that they were thoroughly enjoying it all. There was also a small seal named Tommy who kept interrupting the performance, and two penguins waddling amongst the audience, who were quite enchanting.

We left Port Elizabeth about noon and made our way to East London, a rather monotonous drive through very different country with hills covered in scrub as far as the eye could see. The road was lined with wire fencing on either side, and was dead straight until it entered Grahamstown, once the capital of Settler country, but now a rather quiet University town housing the Rhodes University and several excellent schools. We drove on for East London through the heart of the pineapple growing region. It was very hot and dusty, and we were glad to buy some of the fruit from a native boy by the roadside. On arrival at East London, we booked in at The Kennaway, named after the good ship *Lady Kennaway* which brought a cargo of one hundred and fifty three Irish Colleens in 1837, as prospective brides for the German Legionares who had settled in this area.

During our drive next day through flat country, we passed native kraals for the first time, the huts made of mud with thatched roofs, many of the walls painted with designs in vivid colours. The women wore long loose dresses in gay colours, and carried their loads on their heads walking slowly and gracefully, smiling and waving to us as we passed. We saw two youths walking in the veldt, quite naked, with their bodies painted white. It is the custom for boys at the age of puberty to be sent out into the wild armed only with a spear and a knife, to fend for themselves for a period of time.

East London was very hot and humid, and we were glad to enter the cooler cloudier country of the Traanskei, which made the drive much more enjoyable, passing over vast expanses of gently rolling hills dotted with native villages, the huts gaily painted in red and white. These were farming communities, but the land looked poor and eroded, not supplying much nourishment for their cattle and sheep. Each hut had a patch of maize in front of it: the family's staple diet.

This is known as the "Red Blanket Country", needless to say red is the predominant colour, and the women were smoking long clay pipes. Driving along the vast expanse of nothing, it was puzzling to know where the odd native walking along the verge, was going to or from whence he came.

We arrived at Umtata, the administrative capital of the Traanskei. The light was fading when we arrived at 6 p.m. and it seemed a strange place to find after the vast emptiness through which we had come. The Savoy was a strange hotel too, though we were made very welcome and comfortable despite everything being so hot and sticky.

The mileometer registered exactly one thousand as we left Umtata, and we found we only had one hundred and ten miles to do that day to reach our next port of call – Kokstat. En route we found a pub at Mount Frere, its name, the New Carlton, belied its appearance, and here we quenched our thirst with two bottles of beer each, and had some very good home made steak and kidney pies. The air cooling system was provided by overhead rushes operated by a native pulling a cord. The scenery was very much the same as yesterday, but the villages became larger, the agricultural efforts better, and the grass greener, and so we arrived at Kokstat. There was absolutely nothing to see or do here, it was Frank's choice, his reason being that he had never been there, and he had his leg pulled unmercifully as we looked forward to our departure from the soulless town. We chatted to two young girls who were travelling on their own in a decrepit second hand car, and they had to be sure they carried a good supply of bottled water to keep the radiator topped up! One was from Derby and the other from Manchester. They had left home four years before and taken jobs as secretaries in Cape Town, then in Livingstone, and were on their way to Durban where they hoped to sell their car and travel back to the U.K via Greece. I often wonder if they made it.

We had climbed 4200 feet that day, but were going up to 9000 feet to the Sanai Pass. None of us was sorry to leave Kokstat at 0900 next day after wishing the girls farewell. We had been travelling on tarmac latterly, but the rest of our journey was on dirt roads. It was all so dusty we had to wind up the car windows whenever we saw a car approaching to avoid being choked and covered with dust.

We gained height all the way into and over the Drakensberg range with many twists and turns and came upon the Sanai Pass quite suddenly, and what a surprise it was, nestling in the mountains. The full extent of the buildings were not visible from the road, and it was not until we were shown our quarters, a Rondaavel divided into two and sharing a common thatched roof, that we were able to walk round and explore the grounds.

This place, high up in the wilds, had everything – swimming pool, tennis courts, bowling green, children's playground, a golf course and ponies. What a labour it must have been to get all the necessary materials up here.

We decided, despite the altitude and the heat, to take a walk in these magnificent mountains, and climbed, following a marked trail, to the Bushmen's caves were we found rock paintings. It is incredible to think people actually lived here.

We were glad of a bath and change, and found a delightful lounge where we sat either side of a curved bar and collected drinks from a hatch. After a meal Jess and I took on the menfolk at a game of snooker, neither Jess or I had played the game before, and we became quite hysterical, and unbelievably, we won! Emerging from the main buildings to make our way to our quarters, we were regaled with the most tremendous cacophony of bull frogs and crickets. I had never heard anything like it before, unfortunately the chorus continued most of the night.

We were all a bit loth to leave, and spent some time strolling around the grounds enjoying it all so much, and eventually leaving for Durban in the late morning.

There is nothing to tell of the journey, except that the weather became overcast, and it was actually spitting with rain as we neared Durban – our first rain. The hotel was disappointing as it seemed to accommodate the very elderly, either in wheel chairs, or lame. I recall there was a framed report of The Relief of Mafeking in the bar. Frank and Henry went to the Durban Club to see if there was a report of the Law Society results in The Times. We were anxious to learn of Jonathan's results.

Jess and I enjoyed a visit to the hairdressers, washing out the dust of our travels, and Frank took us as his guests, to the Country Club, a beautiful place to the north of the city, occupying one hundred and twenty seven acres and supplying all the usual amenities, the swimming pool being a necessity as sea bathing was out of the question with strong undercurrents and the danger of sharks. We had Asian waiters who are, incidentally, far more intelligent than the African. Frank drove us outside the city to show us the vast sugar plantations, each having their own mill or two, and their own villages for the Indian labourers. We had tea at the Oyster Bar Umhllanga Rocks, a very sophisticated resort, and, in the harbour, saw the Tanker which suffered a severe explosion, and which killed a friend of Jeremy Rind's. Jem, a friend of ours from Dale, was fortunate to be on leave at the time.

Durban marks the parting of our ways, and we shall miss the company, the trip together has been so happy and enjoyable.

———————————— ⚬⚬ ————————————

SOUTH AFRICA
NATAL, ZULULAND
and RHODESIA

After breakfasting together we saw Frank and Jess off to Bloemfontein, and felt very sad at the parting, but we had the excitement of new adventures to look forward to on our own. We spent a busy day visiting travel agents, car hire people, the A.A and the bank, and later went for a walk along the promenade to the Marine Parade. This was a very disappointing part of Durban, very trippery with fair grounds, boat trips etc. I was trapped by two Rickshaw men in full regalia and had my photograph taken with them either side of me – to my horror – and we had a job to get rid of them. We returned to the travel agents and were delighted to learn that they had been able to book one night at Mbabane in Natal, one in the Kruger park, at Skukuza, and a fourth night at Sabie bungalows outside the reserve.

So, here we are setting off on our own, it being Friday April 10th. The car delivered was a Hillman, and we left Durban in high spirits on the National road through miles and miles of sugar cane. We decided to take a side road which led to Eshowe, the administrative centre for Zululand, a pleasant clean town, where we stopped and called at the tourist office to see if they could tell us where we could see native villages. A charming and helpful girl told us that a friend of hers, a sugar cane farmer (there doesn't seem to be any other kind around here) had a Zulu Kraal on his land, and she telephoned him to see if it was possible for us to pay a visit. So we had lunch of rolls, paté and beer, and set off on the route she had mapped out for us. It was a dreadful road, in fact no more than a rough track, with sugar cane six ft high either side We could see nothing except this winding track, and very nearly turned back, but suddenly, on rounding a bend, we came to a clearing at the top of a rise, and there was a lovely bungalow surrounded by a very English looking garden, and a young man in shorts came out to greet us introduced himself as Graham Stewart and offered us tea before taking us to the Kraal. He was preserving this and the Zulu way of life, for it is fast disappearing with civilization encroaching rapidly, and I expect, by now, it is probably a tourist attraction, if it still exists.

A visit to the Kraal

The Kraal was only about two hundred yards from Graham's bungalow, in scrubland and surrounded by a thorn bush fence. We were introduced to the chief, an old man squatting on the ground, who chatted to us, and on translation by Graham, we learned it was a speech of welcome to his humble Kraal. We too made a courtesy speech of thanks and we all shook hands. We were shown two granaries, which were deep holes in the ground with very smooth linings made from cow dung. As we were walking around the beehive shaped huts, a magnificent Zulu emerged from one, dressed in skins(which looked a bit tatty, and smelt a bit too), but his feathered headdress was beautiful, and after a discussion with the chief, they performed a dance for us. We sat on a plank supported by tree stumps, eight maidens wearing nothing but strings of beads and a few feathers appeared, all smiles, and danced for us accompanied by a few instruments and drums. The girls were joined by men brandishing spears and the famous Zulu shield, and a young matron standing apart from the dancers ululating in a beautiful voice. The girls left the men to show off their athletic prowess, and even the old chief joined in to prove that he was quite capable still. All this was translated to us by Graham, I do not describe it at all well, but the rhythm, the stamping, the singing and the colour were all so exciting.

We were invited by the young matron, who was very beautiful incidentally, to enter her hut, and this we did by stooping very low, and were surprised at the spaciousness and the cleanliness, especially when told that cow dung was used to polish the floor, it being spread on and dampened every two to three weeks. There were a few skins spread over it and sleeping mats rolled up on one side, with wooden neck rests. The cooking utensils were all made of clay, and there was a hole in the apex of the thatched roof for the smoke to escape. We expressed our grateful thanks and bade them all farewell. Writing it now it all seems like a dream.

We made our way down the dusty track to the road again, very hot and dusty, and made for the Hluhluwe – pronounced Shishlooee – game reserve, and were delighted to find a swimming pool at The White Rhino hotel, and plunged into it without any ado. We requested tea to be sent to us at 5 a.m. as we wished to be at the gates of the game park as soon as it opened at 6 a.m. This we did and found a family of Americans also waiting. On going through the gates, opened by a smiling warden (these natives are all smiles), the sun was rising, a great orange sphere which lit everything with a fiery glow, and the first game we saw silhouetted against this sunrise, was a huge herd of buffalo, a fearsome looking lot, said to be more dangerous than lion, and who will charge at great speed. We passed by these and made our way to the lodge in the centre of the park, our object was to see the rare white rhino, and as our time was limited, we thought it better to have a guide if possible. We found one who spoke no English and understood very little, but he registered that we wished to see the white rhino. We drove a further ten miles passing zebra, kudu, nyala, warthog, and baboon, and came upon the huge beasts. Having a guide with us we were allowed to get out of the car and approach them. They are not white at all, but I understand that "white" is a derivative of the word meaning wide or square, referring to the lip. There was the inevitable Cattle egret or Tick bird on their backs feeding off insects and even cleaning their ears. These are an endangered species, and we were fully satisfied with what we had seen in our limited time, and made our way back to the hotel for a good breakfast.

We pressed on as we had a room booked in Mbabane in Swaziland. This was an uninteresting journey, and a very hot dusty drive, and we travelled most of the two hundred miles on earth roads in temperatures of 90 degrees. The back seat was covered with red dust despite the fact we had tried to prevent it entering the car by closing the windows whenever another car passed. We soon found that 40 mph was a reasonable speed to maintain, and to keep well behind a vehicle rather than try to pass. There were many salutations exchanged by passing traffic, if one had the same make of car, or the same registration (Cape Town), or maybe just liking ones looks, which is indicative of the amount of traffic we encountered.

The Holiday Inn was our destination, and the Zulu boy had to dust our luggage on taking it out of the boot, we even found it had penetrated the cases, so you can imagine what our hair was like! There is no colour bar here, and we found ourselves rubbing shoulders with natives in the bar.

Next day we were on dirt roads again making for Barberton, and the seventy four miles took us three and one half hours, travelling through precipitous mountain passes. One could not take the road at more than 15 mph, but this gave one the time to appreciate the most spectacular views. I took the wheel through this period, and poor Henry was biting his nails. We crossed the border again and entered the town of Havelock, built especially for the workers in the Asbestos mines. Their little bungalows were built in tiers on the hillside, painted blue, pink, cream and white, looking quite attractive. The border police told us they had all amenities too. The company had built an overhead railway to carry the Asbestos, and we followed this for miles and miles and never saw the end. After passing through a tremendous forestry plantation, we eventually drove through the gates of the Kruger park, and a further two miles to the office where we registered, and a further eight miles to the Skukuze encampment.where a Rondaavel had been booked on our behalf for the night. We had to be in the camp by 6 p.m. and the speed limit was 25 mph. We saw only baboon wildebeest and impala, such pretty graceful creatures, a herd of which leapt across the road in front of the car. After a drink and a wash we went out in search of lion before dusk, but only saw four giraffe.

The Kruger is South Africa's largest and one of its oldest National Parks. It began in the last century as the small Sabie Game Reserve and was given National Park status and Paul Kruger's name in 1926. One of its early game wardens was an Englishman – James Stevenson Hamilton, regarded as the father of the present day park. Because of his dedication and his pursuit of poachers, his African trackers named him *Skukuza* – he who sweeps clean. Skukuza is now the main settlement for the park. The whole covers a huge area, over five million acres, the south boundary being the Crocodile River, the east being the border to Mozambique, and the north, the Limpopo river. It is extremely well run, the wildlife being studied and protected, and to a certain extent, the animals managed, which prevents some species from becoming too numerous and squeezing out the weaker ones. We had as much satisfaction from the dazzling array of birds, such as hornbills, eagles, hornbill kingfishers and lilac breasted rollers as we did from the mammals. We were up at 5 a.m. next day having had a very poor night caused by baboons investigating the dustbins, and the roaring of lion, which sounded alarmingly close. We went through the camp gates at 6 a.m. and from then on had an exciting time picking out and following the tracks of animals and saw five lion and two elephant before breakfast – which we had at Lower Sabie, alongside the Sabie river. A round trip arriving back at Skukuze for lunch was followed by a visit to the hippo pool, which was rather disappointing as we only saw the snouts and ears of the beasts when they occasionally emerged. The heat was terrific, and all sensible folk rest between noon and 3 p.m. in the shade, if they can find any. We quenched our thirst and left the Kruger via the Numba gate on the south west border, having driven one hundred and sixty miles in the park and seen so many animals. Impala are everywhere, waterbuck, bushbuck, kudu, nyala, wildebeest, mongoose, warthog, crocodile, lion and my favourite, the elephant. We crossed the Sabie river, which was very shallow, but is a rushing torrent in the rainy season, and arrived at the Sabi bungalows, very tired, dusty and thirsty, had a very welcome bath and drink, and were called to dinner by the sound of a Tom-tom.

Next day we travelled along a beautiful smooth tarmac road, but alas, only for half an hour, when it suddenly became an unmade road seething with natives and machines, and we almost became stuck in the sand, fortunately there were plenty of willing hands to push us free, and this state continued for twenty-five miles. We were very thankful to get onto a good solid road again, and this was really wonderful rising to over seven thousand feet over the Drakensberg mountains (Dutch for the mountain of the dragon) and through Long Tom Pass. One cannot find words to describe the magnificence of the mountain views, and we tried to imagine the Voortrekkers crossing them with their ox driven wagons and no road. Once over the heights, we dropped very little and travelled the flat uninteresting high veldt area, through another world altogether, with fewer native huts, larger agricultural areas, then an industrial belt, and eventually entered the city of Johannesburg, which was dreadful, and found our hotel, the Kempton Park, which was unimpressive, with alteration work taking place.

Here Henry handed over the car to the agents, the milometer registering 1075 miles, and the hotel drove us to the airport next day, which was a seething mass. We boarded a Vickers Viscount, and had a very pleasant flight to Bulawayo, where we all had to alight to go through customs, and only twelve of us went on board again to continue the flight to Victoria Falls. The air hostess pointed to what looked like a bush fire in the distance, but proved to be the spray from the falls, which the natives call"the smoke that thunders" I enjoyed the whole flight. A bus collected us at the airport and drove us to the hotel, where we arrived in a thunderstorm, the first real downpour we had experienced in South Africa. The Victoria Falls hotel was delightful, with an air of restful elegance. We had a spacious room with mosquito nets on the twin beds – the first time I had encountered these. We were glad of the opportunity to stretch our legs, and donning old clothes and macintoshes, went out to explore. Walking along the road signposted The Falls. (One could not really miss them), we came within view of the Zambian border, and turned left through the Rain Forest, through jungle growth with baboons chattering and swinging all about us, and came to the falls. I cannot describe this fantastic spectacle, we just stood and gazed in awe and wonder. We could not see the full length of the falls as the spray rose in great clouds obliterating the view, and forcing great waves of heat around us. We walked back realising that this was only a taste of what was in store for us on the morrow. We were soaked, but after a bath and change, the storm having passed, we enjoyed drinks on the stoep and were accosted by a fellow passenger on the Vaal. We rose after spending a poor night, it being so hot and sticky, and another heavy thunderstorm occurring and disturbances from the ancient plumbing. We breakfasted in a vast dining room reminiscent of former grand days, and found, to our surprise that we were the only ones to be collected by a huge native, named Stanley, but he collected four others from another hotel, so the six of us set off on the tour, first to see a show village of the Matabele tribe, which was very interesting, but one felt, slightly phoney. We were shown the Chief's hut, and those of his three wives, the hen hut and the cattle kraal. The women were pounding corn and maize, and the men painting or carving, a lot of these crafts had been introduced by the missionaries. A number of them, both men and women, were working on basket and leather goods, but what intrigued us most was the carving of the local soapstone, and I could not resist buying the head of a native about three inches high, which I still have. Some natives danced a rather evil dance, wearing most grotesque masks, all of which depicted something, but I knew not what. We were introduced to the Baobab tree, a strange tree that looks as though it is growing upside down with its roots in the air, this one was reputed to be two thousand years old. We went on to what we had come to see, "the smoke that thunders".

Although it was a lovely clear day, we certainly needed our waterproofs as we walked through the forest to each view point to gaze at the spectacle, and emerged soaked to the skin from the spray. We walked over the bridge, or rather half way across, as there was a no man's land of about two yards in the centre, and were advised not to step across, as the sentry on the Zambian border would have no hesitation in using his firearm! We gazed at the churning mass of water below, the depth of which is unknown as no instrument survives the waters. The width of the river is 1860 yards and the height of the falls three hundred and four feet, and was discovered in 1855, as everyone knows, by Dr. David Livingstone, whose statue stands nearby. From the hotel grounds one has a wonderful view of the famous horseshoe shape of the river with the rainbow suspended over all.

After a drying out session and a light lunch, we were driven to a spot about two miles upriver where we boarded a steamer which took us a pleasant sail to an island, seeing hippos en route, where we disembarked and went ashore penetrating jungle and rested in the shelter of a wooden hut with an open front. The deck hands brought us tea and biscuits, and we were soon surrounded by scores of small monkeys, I think they were Vervats, who were full of mischief and obviously used to visitors and expected a share of our tea. One of the party had his spectacles snatched from off his nose, and the retrieving of these by the boys provided great entertainment. I felt the heat terribly, and was glad to get on board again where the movement of the boat provided a slight breeze. Back at the hotel we relaxed in the shade on the stoep.

This is a beautiful country with such a variety of scenery and peoples, all of whom seem so happy and cheerful, and I have never seen anything so spectacular as the Falls. We were taken to a small airstrip next day, and boarded a very

43

decrepit looking Dakota for a flight to Kariba. I was terrified, especially when we ran into a terrific storm and the pilot was dubious as to whether he would be able to land at Wankie to pick up four passengers. However, he made it, but we were grounded for some time waiting for the storm to abate. Eventually we took off for an hour's flight to Kariba and flew over the Dam. On landing, we were taken to sign in at The Cutty Sark, photographing an elephant conveniently browsing by the roadside. The storm passed and we sat outside on the stoep overlooking the lake watching the lightning flashing in all directions in a most spectacular fashion, with the temperatures in the 90's. We both felt this was a visit we could have done without, and omitted going to the dam and the crocodile farm, curling up with a book instead. Back again at the airport, we boarded another Dakota, not such a decrepit one thank goodness, and took off for Salisbury. The Captain told us to fasten our seat belts after flying about fifteen minutes, as we were approaching another storm, fortunately he managed to skirt the huge black cloud, and the lights of Salisbury twinkled prettily below and we landed at about 6 p.m. We said farewell to our companions with no great regret, and went to Miekels hotel, where we found a letter from Frank saying there was a lot of mail for us in Cape Town, but none, he thought, from Jonathan, which was the one we were anxiously waiting for.

---------------------------------- C3&O ----------------------------------

MOZAMBIQUE

The next day was full of incident, the first being an extraordinary coincidence. As we were walking through the foyer of the hotel, a figure rose from a deep armchair and greeted us by name, who should it be but Chris Redfern, who at that time was working for Dr. Banda in Malawi. He was on his way to Durban to collect his car which had been damaged in transit on his return to Malawi from leave, and which he had had to leave in Durban to be repaired. We had last seen Chris during his leave at Dale, and admired his car which we named his "Crumpet Catcher". It was amazing that we should meet in those few minutes.

Our car was waiting outside, a BMW this time, and we set off for Mozambique. We were truly impressed with all the arrangements the travel agents had made for us, so far everything had gone like clockwork. Not so today, but nothing to do with the agents, we had a puncture two miles out of Umtali, and, fortunately for us, a car containing three brawny Rhodesians drew up and offered assistance.

We had to stop at the border and register our departure from Rhodesia and, a few yards on, our entrance into Portuguese South Africa, and then pressed on for Gorongoza. Visitors had to be within the gates of the Game Park by 1730. Unfortunately we missed the turning and had to retrace our tracks. We found the turning – unsignposted.

It was a shocking unmade road, and Henry tore along it with me hanging on for dear life. After about eleven miles of this hair-raising drive we rounded a bend to find a stationary car, with the owner – a German – paddling in a river apparently testing the depth. There were no apparent means of crossing the river, which, on the map looked a fordable trickle. The German spoke very little English, and the other two people present were African and spoke no English. One of them gave us a blank stare, and the other a cheery grin, and proceeded to undress and wash his clothes in the water. As we were wondering what to do, a lorry loaded with soldiers drew up, and fortunately, the Sergeant spoke understandable English. He explained that the bridge had been swept away, that he and his men had been instructed to repair it, and would start work in the morning.

"How long will it take?" we asked.

Our pontoon across the swollen river

Shrugging his shoulders he replied, "Eight, nine, ten days, who knows? This is Africa."

We drove back along the horrendous track again, by which time the light was going rapidly. Rather than return to Rhodesia we decided to strike east for the port of Beira, and try for accommodation. We found a hotel, and after breakfast, visited the Tourist Bureau, where a plump maiden by the name of Venus Mary obligingly phoned through to the Reserve to see what was happening. As this was going to take a little while, we walked round the port. We were not impressed with Beira, it all looked a bit grubby, and the buildings most flamboyant. On our return, Venus Mary told us that a ferry of sorts was being organised, but we might have to wait.

Off we set for the two hour drive back to the river crossing, and were quite horrified to see the state of the road over which we had driven in the dark. It was a narrow strip of tarmac in the centre, with rough unmade track either side to enable one to pass vehicles, with a drop to the river with no fencing.

On arrival at the river, we saw the ferry returning from the opposite bank, with a small bus on board. Waiting on our side was a yellow pick-up truck, and a car full of Americans who had been waiting half an hour. The bus eventually landed, and was immediately filled with chattering, laughing natives, and sacks of Millet were unloaded and put on a waiting lorry. The pick-up and the Americans boarded, leaving no room for us, and we watched, fascinated, as the pontoon pushed off guided through the currents by natives wielding huge bamboo poles. We were entertained during our wait, by a native who unzipped a bag, withdrew a blanket and various clothing and some soap, and proceeded to wash them all in the river, pounding them with his feet, and spreading them out on the bushes to dry. Some children came to the water to fish, and appeared to flick the fish out of the river with their hands. The army had erected a pontoon of sorts, but it was not in use as the river was far too high and still rising. We eventually boarded, having waited over an hour, and our crew of seven worked their long poles to propel us through the currents around small islands, dipping filthy cans into the muddy waters to quench their thirst – no wonder they

47

suffer from Bilhartzia, but they were a cheery lot who sang as they poled. The crossing took three quarters of an hour and we eventually landed, and drove off for the Reserve, with natives waving us a send off.

We drove through the park gates and on to the camp, a matter of seventeen kms, and en route saw a herd of ten elephants. Our Rondavaal was built to house two parties with a communal bathroom, in which we found pink frogs hopping about, which put me off a bit. A native supplied us with hot water by lighting a fire under a boiler outside the bathroom, and we had lovely hot water in a surprisingly short time. Things were made a little difficult when the lights fused, but these things happen even at the Savoy. After a meal of good soup, tasty fish, and shocking beef (we suspected buffalo) accompanied by a pleasant Portuguese wine, we were ready for bed intending to rise early.

We left camp about 6.15 a.m. and even then found we were about the last of the twenty four guests to leave. At the gate we asked for an English speaking guide, and were provided with a huge native by the name of Matube, and the conversations was, "left here." "Right here." "Stop." "Back a lot." "Yes Massa." He addressed me as "My lady" or "Mudder". He knew his animals all right, and could speak far more English than we could Portuguese.

We saw a tremendous variety of game and in larger numbers than previously. On the plain, zebra, buck and wildebeest abounded, together with lion and elephant. The birds were plentiful and exotic, but Matube was not so knowledgeable on our feathered friends as he was on the animals.

At About 11.30 p.m. we said, "no more thank you, back to camp," and we were glad to sit and have a drink before lunch in the company of some Californians. This searching for animals, who are all so well camouflaged, can be quite exhausting. We made arrangements to travel in the company of some Rhodesians after siesta, in search of lion, and were most fortunate in finding about eight lioness browsing in the ruins of some disused concrete huts, together with more cubs than we could count, as they played and frolicked with each other, and we returned to camp completely satisfied with all that we had seen during the day.

The Americans and Rhodesians planned to leave camp at 6 a.m. and as the ferry only took two vehicles at a time, we decided to leave about 8 a.m. We were told that a cattle truck at the ferry took precedence over private cars, and Army trucks had priority over cattle trucks, and so we prepared for a long wait, and armed ourselves with a pack of cards and a flask of coffee. We did have quite a long wait, arriving in time to see the ferry leave, and on the return, the polers decided to have a rest and a drink, then a lorry of grain arrived and the sacks had to be man-handled on board. Eventually we drove on board the flimsy craft, and had the company of ten natives who sang and chanted during the crossing. One small boy kept peering into our car, but was too shy to accept my invitation to enter. On landing, we gave a Mozambique policeman a lift to his village, and passed through acres of flax grown by a textile company, before dropping our friend, and crossing the border at Umtali. We decided to try our luck for a bed somewhere in the Vumba Mountains.

It was a most enjoyable drive, climbing all the time and passing through lovely country and coffee growing estates, and we came upon the Highland Lodge Hotel, 6000 ft up. It had the appearance of an English inn, with thatched roof and leaded windows, and inside we were welcomed with the sight of a log fire. We had a spacious room with cretonne soft furnishings, rose covered wallpaper, a beautiful view, and a hot water bottle in our beds. Such comforts were bliss after roughing it, and we met some interesting people, two of whom had lived in South Africa and Rhodesia for forty years and who came from Goodwick Pembs originally, and a Scot who had retired early and come to live in Zambia. The air was sharp and cool, a pleasant change from the heat of the plains.

On leaving Highland Lodge we passed through the National Park, which was beautifully landscaped with ornamental lakes and streams, with banks of Hydrangea, Azalia, Protea and Poinsettia, the latter growing wild by the roadside, and so many birds which were a joy to see.

SOUTH AFRICA
JOHANNESBURG GOLD MINES
BLUE TRAIN TO CAPE TOWN

We stopped at a small town – Machade – and called in the one and only hotel where we sat on high stools at the bar, and were entertained by the landlord and three customers, one of whom was a Welshman from Carmarthen who had come out twenty years ago with the princely sum of two thousand pounds to farm. We had a very interesting discussion on the state of our countries and politics in general, and having put the world to rights, they gave us a terrific send-off.

We entered Salisbury in the late afternoon and delivered the car to the hire firm, and strolled through the city, which was quite delightful with the main street lined with Jacaranda in full bloom. At the hotel we contacted Ray and Phil Lamb, friends of Frank and Jessie's whom we had met in Cape Town, fulfilling our promise to get in touch with them. We did not make a date, pleading fatigue. It poured with rain during dinner, when it does rain here it pelts down.

Next day, on arrival at the airport, we found our flight had been cancelled and were told there might be one at 2.45 p.m., so, finding ourselves at a loose end, we again contacted Ray Lamb, who, bless her, immediately cancelled her engagements and took charge of us, driving us first to a Kopje overlooking the city, where she pointed out places of interest, including the huge Tobacco warehouses which Phil owned. We then went through the University campus, and eventually to her lovely home, a long low building built in

51

two sections, one for them and the other for the servants, joined together by a pergola covered with Jacaranda, and standing in two acres of beautifully kept gardens. No problem with domestic staff here! We met the gardener and the cook, and they appeared to be very happy indeed.

We were so grateful to Ray for entertaining us at such short notice.

Back again at the airport, there was still no flight, which was all a bit frustrating, but the officials were very apologetic, and telephoned our hotel in Johannesburg telling them of the delay, and we returned to Meikels.

On Saturday April 25th we made it, and flew to Johannesburg in a Boeing 707. I am beginning to enjoy flying! After a long wait for an airport bus, and another for a taxi to the hotel, we were more than a bit browned off to find the place full of workmen and a great deal of banging in progress, as though they were in the process of rebuilding the whole place. Our small room was not at all welcoming, and the telephone did not work, but, we told ourselves, it was only for two nights, and we would be out most of the next day.There was, however, a welcome letter from Jonathan, but no news yet of exam results, but telling us that Hugh was at Dale on study leave. There was also a message from a Mr.Posnett, an agent of Slip Mennel's the owner of the gold mines we met in Cape Town, saying he would collect us 8.15 a.m. to take us to the Mine dances, and later entertain us to lunch at the Bryanston Club, which all sounded very promising.

We walked into the city hoping to finish off a film in the camera and to get a new supply of film, only to find the shops shut. Fortunately we found a chemist open for prescriptions and were able to buy some.

We were unimpressed with Johannesburg, it all looked so dirty after the beautiful country we had been through, and maybe it was the effect of everything being closed. There was a sinister atmosphere about the city too, and we were glad to return to the shelter of our sordid hotel and retire early as we had to be up in good time next day.

Sunday April 26th was a memorable day indeed. We had no idea what our hosts would be like, and of course, neither did they have any idea what we were like. They were a delightful young couple and we all got on famously.

They collected us after early breakfast and drove us through the mining area with its mountains of golden waste at the pit heads, coco pans moving slowly along the rails, and Africans everywhere.

The camp itself must have covered a vast area with its playing fields for the workers, its shopping centre, houses for the Europeans, and a village of long shed-like buildings for the miners. We remarked on these, and were told they were very comfortable inside, the men being provided with every comfort, and were far better off than in their kraals. I wondered about this, and am sure that the introduction of even a little of our way of life, must create some discontent. It is considered a status symbol among the young girls of the kraal for the young men to do a spell of work in the mines, and they return after a period of labour driving their very own albeit very decrepit cars, and after living a life of ease say, for six months, they return to the mines.

At the dance centre, we sat on stone benches built in tiers around an earth circle where the dances were performed. Three hundred and fifty thousand Africans work here on contract for two to three years, men from fifty different tribes some of whom are life long enemies, and the dances are performed by men from a different mine each Sunday, specifically to work off their surplus energy, which, otherwise might well be engaged in tribal fights. They make their own instruments and costumes, and perform their own dances entirely for their own enjoyment, and we, the audience are permitted to watch by invitation only. The

Africans are natural dancers, and they were all fantastic. Some of the dresses were their own tribal costume, ostrich feathers abounding, and one party entered the arena wearing wellington boots and jeans and played harmonicas.

There was in interval for tea, for which we were very grateful, the stone seats were very hard. We left about noon, and our hosts took us to their Country Club for lunch, all of which was very pleasant, then a drive around Pretoria to see the government buildings, then back to their home for tea. We invited them to be our guests for dinner at The President, and retired about 10.30 p.m. late for us, after a most interesting and pleasant day.

Johannesburg began life as a mining camp in 1886 when rich gold deposits were first discovered, and has grown at a phenomenal rate, and is now the largest city in South Africa. Links with the early gold rush days are evident in the names of the streets – Claim, Quartz, Nugget etc. Paul Kruger, its President in the 1890's did a great deal in the shaping of the city, and of Pretoria as the seat of the government and a noted educational centre.

I would have liked to have explored to the north of the city where the Voortrekkers blazed a trail early in the 19th century, taking years to achieve this in their ox-wagons. One party came to a north flowing river, and believed they had discovered the source of the Nile, where they established the little town of Nylstroom, and area rich in history.

We had heard a great deal about the "Blue Train"and were told travel on this was an experience not to be missed. We were not sorry to leave Johannesburg, and boarded this famous train at 10 a.m. On Monday April 27th. We had a comfortable cabin with twin bunks, a shower and toilet. There was a well appointed communal lounge and dining area, and an open viewpoint at the rear of each carriage.

The morning's scenery was dull and flat for miles and

miles. At Kimberley, the engine was changed from diesel to steam, and being in the first carriage, it shook and shuddered until 2.30 a.m. when we once again transferred to diesel. On rising at 7.a.m. we were surprised to find that it was only just getting light, and were delighted to see hills which developed into mountains during breakfast, through which we twisted and turned like a long snake, often seeing the end carriage of the train, and, losing height, gradually entered the De Droon Valley with acres and acres of vines, then across the great Karoo desert.

Jessie and Frank were at Cape Town to meet us, and the first thing they did was to hand us a telegram from Jonathan, which had arrived that very morning, telling us the good news that he had passed his law exams. We could not have had a more joyous welcome.

There was a great re-union with so much to tell, and letters from Jonathan, Hugh and Ellinor to read. We had been so looking forward to hearing from them all.

SOUTH AFRICA
CAPE TOWN and VOYAGE HOME

We are nearing the end of our holiday, and there is still a lot to do and see. Frank wanted to show us the area of Tulbegh and Ceres which suffered an earthquake the previous September, and was still feeling slight tremors daily. There were houses beyond repair, prefabricated houses erected and tents in most gardens. Friction from falling stones from the surrounding mountains had set alight to escaping gas causing serious fires

Leaving this area we went through a wonderful pass on a narrow road, with a deep drop on one side and overhanging rocks on the other called Baines Kloof, named after a surveyor in 1840. There we had lunch, then dropped to the river which was normally fast flowing, but it was all so dry we only saw the occasional clear pool with water just trickling through the boulders.

That evening we spent a very pleasant time showing our slides on a projector and screen that John and Trish brought with them. Granny particularly enjoyed those of Rhodesia. The weather had changed, and we enjoyed a log fire in the evening, and when walking on the contour line of Table mountain, were glad of woollies.

We hosted Frank and Jess for lunch at The Mount Nelson. I had heard a great deal about this hotel from Henry, he had visited it on previous business trips, and it came up to my expectations. A very elegant dining room indeed, with high ceilings, crystal chandeliers, blue and gold drapes, and the waiters wearing white gloves!

We went to lunch one day with Frank and Jess, to Lanzerac, one of the original dutch farmhouses in Stellenbosch, run by two brothers from the U.K. named Rawdon. We sat outside on the stoep in the sunshine enjoying our drinks, then had a superb meal indoors during which I was puzzling over the familiar face of a gentleman having a meal in the company of two others. Eventually I was able to put a name to him – Prof. Patrick Moore, the Astrologist who appears regularly on Television at home in a series *The Sky at Night*. Nothing deters Jess, who immediately approached the men as they were leaving their table. Frank, realising what she was about muttered, "Oh my God!" and disappeared into the Gents toilet. Jess explained that her cousin from the U.K had recognised him, and he came across to us, obviously delighted, and was quite charming. He was just as he appears on the screen, rather like an overgrown untidy schoolboy with his collar sticking out and his tie awry. He was in Stellenbosch recording a series of lectures for the University.

On our return to Mulvihal Road, we found a message from Royce Bowen inviting us to have a drink with them, so Henry and I borrowed Jess's car and drove to their house, and from there we were taken to the Great bear, which is the equivalent of The Woodlands at the Pontypool plant, a place for entertaining VIP customers. Here we found several of the South African Nylon Spinners people assembled to bid us farewell and bon voyage. We did not stay long as we wished to spend our last night with the Wooddisse family, and there was packing to be done.

On Wednesday, May 6th, we said sad farewells to Robert, Grannie, Lizzie – who wept copiously – Inca, and the Table Mountain with its cloth of mist.

It is strange recounting our trip twenty years later, so much has happened in the country. We did visit it again in

1978 and noticed quite a number of changes then, but now President De Klerk has released Mandela from twenty years incarceration on Robben Island, many restrictions on blacks have been lifted, and there is talk of one man one vote.

I am glad apartheid has been abolished, and I wonder if Mandela will ever become President.

We were ready to leave and Frank and Jess drove us to the docks to board the Edinburgh Castle, very nearly her last voyage, as the Mail line is closing down, and, I suppose, Air Lines will be taking over – the end of an era.

We met in the Smoke room after seeing our luggage installed in our cabin, and of course, found Frank already in conversation with a friend from Constantia, a widower travelling on his own to London. We had a last drink with Frank and Jess, who did not stay long, and the farewells were short, which is the best way.

We shall treasure very happy memories of the time we spent with them, and the kindness they have shown, all of which we hope to reciprocate next year, when they plan to visit us.

We made our way to our cabin to unpack and to meet our steward named Pyne, and met the head steward in the Dining saloon, who placed us at the Purser's table, together with his wife and two middle aged ladies, sisters-in-law, named Sutcliffe, who were a bit stuffy.

I was the only one at our table for breakfast next morning, after a very blowy night with gale force seven winds and a severe roll on the liner, and spent some time on deck, although it was quite a job to find a sheltered spot out of the wind and spray. I chatted to a lady from Falmouth who joined me. She and her husband had a Land Rover on board in which they had had a wonderful trip through South Africa. It was fitted with extra tanks for petrol and had a built in safe, and Swahili for "drunken traveller" painted on the side, which, apparently, caused great amusement among the natives wherever they went.

So life on board took over, with its competitions in Quoits, Bowls etc, and our ritual of a mile before breakfast, which was eight times round the deck. We visited the Bridge at the invitation of the Captain, who, of course, knew Frank, and we entered into everything quite well and happily, although it was not our   scene, and we entered the tropics leaving the Cape winds behind us.

We soon met people, two of whom from Shell knew the Whiteheads, and it was from them that we learnt that Christine had left Gerry, and had gone to the U.K to take up residence with Colin Bagnall, the Director of B.N.S. Charles, our steward, puts Henry's shirt, dinner jacket, shoes etc out each evening, and I feel I should ask him to select a gown for me, but the choice is rather limited.

The Doctor and the Padre, both Irish, were good fun, and the latter addresses all females as "me darling."

We had the company of two Albatross flying with us for four days.

There was a dance or discotheque each evening, but with the temperature in the 80's, it was more pleasant to be on deck watching the phosphorence on the water. We were now in the Doldrums, and despite the heat, managed to play off our mixed double finals in Bowls, which we lost, even though we had to play the last point again, the pucks being dead level. Among the interesting people we met, there was a Rev Justice Mort who had resigned from the Milawi courts, the fourth Justice to have done so through disagreements with the government, he was going to enter the church in U.K.

There was a Cattle Ranch manager who worked for Fray Bentos, and told us the only way he could check the cattle was by riding the vast estate on horseback which took him ten to fourteen days; a Civil Engineer who had been building roads in Kenya, but after his leave was going to join a private concern in Zambia;a coloured couple who were travelling around the world at the expense of his employer – a builder – as a reward for having worked for him for fifty two years.

The nonsensical ceremony of "crossing the line" was held, after which the sea was the smoothest I had ever seen it, incredible to think that it is two miles deep.

Soon we left the tropics and a breeze developed which turned into a strong wind and whipped off the head-scarf I was wearing, and, needless to say we shall not be having any more buffet lunches on deck, and on the morrow, we expect to see land.

We put into Las Palmas at 09.30 and were advised to lock our cabins when leaving them, and were not surprised when we saw the odd looking characters milling around. It was good to stretch our legs on terra firma. Unfortunately, I was very sick on returning to the cabin, apparently there was a bug going around affecting quite a number of passengers, and I could not face anything to eat for twenty-four hours.

We were happy that the end of our voyage was not too far away, and one could sense an eager expectancy among the passengers. In the Bay of Biscay we put our watches on one hour. The sea seemed surprisingly calm, and we hoped it would remain so all night.

Sunday May 17the was our last day afloat, and it dragged terribly. We were all anxious to get ashore, but were told there would be a delay in landing owing to a meeting of the Stevedore's Union at 0800 tomorrow, with a strike in view.

We had a convivial party with the friends we had made on board, but we were all itching to get ashore and see our relatives and friends. It was a lovely calm day, but nowhere to sit on deck as all the chairs had been stored, the games cleared away, and the pool emptied, so there was nothing to do but drink.

The good news next day was that the strike had not materialised, and we made our way through the hubbub of the customs and onto the boat train. Oh! how lovely and green everywhere looked. The lilacs were in full bloom, there is nowhere like England in the spring, and it was good to be back, but it will take some time to settle down to the quiet life in Dale, although Henry will be starting a Consultancy appointment in Bury of all places.

What a wonderful experience our trip has been, the memories of which will last for ever.

FRANCE and SPAIN 1972

We had a busy time after our trip to South Africa, house hunting, and the prospect of 3 weddings. We purchased the Old Vicarage at Llanvair Kilgeddin to which we made a number of alterations, removed our furniture from store, and installed ourselves in our new abode which we renamed "Glebe House", and coped with 3 weddings. All this took place in 1971, and we were quite ready for a holiday. We had an invitation from George Carey – a friend of Gwyn Sproule Jones – who had befriended Jonathan whilst he was studying at the Law College in Guildford. He was a director of Sandeman's, and suggested we went to the Douro in Portugal for the vintage in October. The idea appealed to us immensely, and we decided to take the car and drive through France and Spain to arrive in Oporto at the end of September.

We left home on Thursday September 14th and had a good run to Southampton, where we filled the tank before boarding the ferry, petrol being less expensive here than in France. On arrival at Cherbourg we drove straight to Granville, but to our dismay could not get a room there and were advised to go on to Julloville, a further 7 kilos to Hotel du Casino, where we had a nice room and an evening meal.

We made for the Loire valley next day, stopping to admire the wonderful view of the bay overlooking Mont. St. Michael, and pulled in at Avanches to do some shopping. On arrival at Amboise on the Loire, we booked in at France et Cheval Blanc, and found, to our horror, that my toilet case, which contained my travellers cheques and a little jewellery, was missing. The landlady was so kind, and telephoned the hotel at Juloville, and we were relieved to learn that they had the case in safe keeping. Needless to say we were very depressed at this poor beginning and sick with ourselves for being so stupid. We left for Juloville after breakfast, and I drove the one hundred and eighty nine kilos. We collected the case all intact and Henry drove back to Amboise. We decided to put this unfortunate incident behind us and enjoy our holiday from then on, and be more careful!

We wandered round this pleasant market town, then drove south to Chemmamceaux, and spent the entire afternoon visiting the lovely Chateau, then planned our route for the next day.

We were finding France expensive, and were exceeding our budget, but hoped that Spain and Portugal would be cheaper and help to balance out.

We cut across country to the Dordogne to find a hotel that Tim Sandeman had recommended at Lot, but we could not find it, and could not get any assistance on enquiring at Perigueux, so decided to stay the night at Les Eyzies.

This turned out to be quite a tourist centre, with prehistoric caves being the main attraction, which, of course we visited, the latter part of the visit being by boat. The mosquitoes were abundant, and Henry, poor thing, suffered badly.

We had travelled two hundred and seventy miles, so decided to have an easier day, and on leaving Les Eyzies I took the wheel until lunch, and although I enjoyed the driving I handed over to Henry as he was far too scared for some reason.

Passing through some lovely country and delightful villages, we came upon Lot and found the recommended hotel, where we booked in for the night and enjoyed a superb meal.

We left Lot with the intention of staying at Dax, but found it too industrial for our liking, and drove out and selected a hotel which, unfortunately, proved to be a bad choice. After a meal and retiring, something disagreed with me and I had to make a long trek to a WC twice during the night, and we could not get out of the place quick enough. I was feeling very groggy and it poured with rain. We found our way across the border, avoiding the coast road on the advice of Harry Judge (Dale), and climbed and climbed through cloud and rain with only the occasional peep of the landscape. The view would, I am sure, have been fantastic on a good day. We were seen across the border by a cheery Gendarme, and welcomed (?) by a sullen Spaniard. It was still pouring with rain, and we had quite a job to find a spot that wasn't thick with mud, to pull up and have our lunch. Having driven one hundred and eighty five klms, we decided to try a Parador, and found the delightful castle Santo Domingo de la Casarda, and thank goodness! found I was able to enjoy the meal. The paradors are excellent and government run. This one was once a resting place on the Pilgrim's Way across northern Spain from France. We explored the town, a delightful place with narrow picturesque alleys, and a most impressive Cathedral in which one shrine of a saint had symbols of a cock and a hen in silver at his feet, and above another shrine was a live cockerel in a cage.

We left in what looked more promising weather, and made for Burgos, where we strolled round the town and visited the Cathedral, which was far too dark and dismal for our taste, then struck north for Santander, a very old and delightful village. The sun actually shone upon us, and we stayed in another Parador, originally the home of the famous Gils Blas. The place was seething with GB registrations, and we had to sleep in the stables which, although beautifully equipped had no private bathroom and no room service. It rained again which cancelled any thought of a walk before dinner, but spent a pleasant evening in the company of a couple from Watford, he being the manager of the Banco d'Espagna in London, and as he knew the country so well, we decided to follow his advice and make for Ribadeo.

The mileage read one thousand and seven after seven days travel, and we set off for Ribadeo in lovely warm sunshine. The road was slow and tortuous, and at one point, to our astonishment, advancing towards us over the brow of a hill, was a huge pair of antlers, which turned out to be the carcass of a large stag tied to the roof of a car, but it did look most extraordinary.

We decided to take the main road, which was a bad choice, as most of it was under repair, then we climbed and twisted up a mountain road, creeping round hair-pin bends at 5mph, eventually reaching the town of Oviedo, and found it to be an ugly industrial city, which we left hurriedly, and again found ourselves climbing and twisting in the mountains. Although we shared the driving, we arrived at Ribadeo very tired, and disappointed to find a coach load of tourists disgorging and entering the Parador, but there was plenty of room, and we were allotted a very pleasant room with a balcony overlooking the water. We decided to leave the morrow's programme until we had some indication of the weather prospect, and went shopping in the town for cheese, tinned sardines, melon and wine (one hundred and forty Pesetas) our lunch for the next two days. Incidentally, Mr.Peffer whom we had met at Santander, discovered he had left a jacket at this Parador, and asked if we would arrange to have it sent to him, but on talking to the Receptionist, we found it would cost us 4/500 Pesetas, so we decided to take it with us and post it to him on our arrival in England.

We had breakfast in our room next day overlooking the bay, but the sky looked heavy and overcast, and we thought it wise to stick to the coast road, rather than traverse the mountains again. A little way along the coast road, we decided it was all too misty to enjoy, so we took to the mountains again, and this choice turned out to be right for once, and we climbed to two thousand feet, then drove over a plateau, and the road made such good travelling, that we drove to Santiago, Vigo, then to the Parador at Bayonne. This had been a fortification similar to Dale Fort, and it looked lovely in the warm sunshine. We walked the ramparts, took photographs, and looked forward to exploring next day. We thought we might spend a second night here, but as the evening meal was poor we made for the border. Incidentally, we only had one good meal in Spain.

It was overcast again when we left Bayonne, but had promise of a nice day, the sea looking calm and lovely as we took the coast road to Portugal. It was a pity the weather had been so poor on our first visit to Spain, even the cowherds were sheltering under their decrepit umbrellas.

We crossed the Portuguese border about 12.30 a.m. with no trouble, passing beneath two manned guns mounted in caves, and the atmosphere quickly changed, the houses and streets looking cleaner and brighter.

After a picnic lunch, we arrived at Firo, which appeared to be a tourist centre for Horizon holidays. I note that I always seem to refer to other people as "tourists" whereas we look upon ourselves as "visitors"!

Henry telephoned Sandeman's to announce our arrival, and arranged for us to go to Oporto on Wednesday morning, which gave us a whole day to relax. We strolled along the beach, then drove to the nearest town for some cash, only to find the bank closed, but we did find a very pleasant Estalagon, where we had a lovely cold beer, and liked the place so much, stayed for lunch, which consisted of Shellfish Soup, followed by Octopus, and Pork Cutlets.On returning to the hotel, we found that Sandeman's had been trying to contact us, inviting us to lunch the next day. We had a feeling that they had only just connected us with George Carey.

PORTUGAL 1972
The Vintage

The old town of Oporto on the north bank of the Douro is well worth a visit. It has intriguing steep alleys winding through dilapidated houses with red tiled roofs, artisans' workshops, snotty-nosed children playing, and women in voluminous skirts selling fruit, vegetables and sardines, with lines of washing hanging across from side to side, flapping in the breeze.

We made our way across the river to Vila da Gaia, to the warehouses or lodges of Oporto's famous export-Port. On the red tiled roofs are neon signs lighting up the famous names – Taylor, Graham, Cockburn and Sandeman. These names appear too on the sails of the traditional Barco Rabelos on the waterfront, barges which transport the huge barrels.

At Sandeman's we were shown into a spacious reception area and welcomed by a Mr. Sinclair, a man in his late thirties, who, after some pleasant chatter, escorted us round the huge caves. We wandered through ancient cobwebby corridors lined with huge barrels of port ageing in oak. The wine is fortified with brandy before being brought down to Oporto, from whence, in due time, it is shipped abroad.

Here we learnt about "Late Bottled Vintage", "Fine Old Tawny", "Ruby and Crusted Port" and ended up in the tasting room, where we given an aperitif of white port, the first I had ever had, and met Gwyn Jennings, co-director, together with two colleagues. We then sat down to lunch in the company of Mr. & Mrs. Jennings, a Mr. Kendall, Mr. Higgins, and Mr. Symington.

This is very much a British community, with the lodges run by families who have been here for generations. Mr and Mrs Jennings had been up the Douro for the vintage, but had been recalled to Oporto for an important funeral, and were full of apologies that we would be left on our own for a while, but said they had booked us into a Pousada in the Douro en route for Vila Real, and we were invited to be their guests at Casa Sandeman for the vintage. Such hospitality we did not expect, and we left after lunch armed with a bottle of Porto Bianco and one of Ruby, and made our way, following their instructions, to the Pousada, driving through picturesque country and climbing to 2900 ft, taking hair-pin bends galore. We found the Pousada situated on yet another bend on a hill, and fervently hoped the traffic did not run all night. Unfortunately, it did! A fellow guest remarked it was "like sleeping on a race track" with vehicles either changing gear ascending, or with brakes screeching on the descent round the bend. On leaving next day, we climbed even higher to 3000 ft driving slowly to admire the wonderful views, had a picnic lunch, and found Casa Sandeman. Mrs Jennings greeted us welcoming us with our first cup of tea since we left home, taken in a very pleasant lounge overlooking a perfectly wonderful view of hills and yet more hills. Our hosts were entertaining friends for dinner, directors of neighbouring lodges and their wives, one, whose name I cannot recall, was the second husband of the famous Odette Churchill, who was tortured by the Gestapo for her work in the French Resistance during the war. I looked forward to meeting her, but, unfortunately she had excused herself as she was suffering from a tummy upset.

Other guests arrived, and we felt a little awkward, being outsiders, as everyone else was on familiar terms and some related, and we had no dinner dress. However, everyone was very kind. The common subject, of course, was vine growing, and wine producing, which, although, foreign to us, we found very interesting.

We enjoyed a super meal of Hake with a shrimp sauce made with cream and tomato ketchup, meat and vegetables, coffee mousse and peaches, accompanied by a smooth white wine which they produce for their own consumption only, and, of course, the decanter of Port doing its rounds. We retired, very tired, about midnight.

We were awakened by a maid bringing tea at 7.45 a.m. breakfasted with our hosts and Olga, the Secretary, and were left with English newspapers and the view to admire until noon, when Mrs.Jennings took us in her car to a Quinta nearby to meet the manager of the vineyard and his wife, and sat on their patio high above the Douro. It was a beautiful steep valley, with the high banks carved into terraces on which the vines grew, with here and there red-tiled warehouses, across the river with the names "Cockburn's" and "Graham's" whitewashed on the roofs. We were taken onto the terraces to see the pickers at work, and were followed by men coming to collect the filled baskets, led by an Accordionist, men with a permanent stoop having laboured thus all their lives. They emptied the baskets into an electric crusher which sent the minced grapes into a tank where it awaited the treaders.

We returned to Casa Sandeman for lunch, after which we were driven to Sarbrosa to see a mechanical plant about eight years old, where the fermentation took place in what looked like giant percolators, which bubbled and exploded in the vacuum. From there we went on to an ultra modern plant at Regna, where Mr.Jennings had his head office during the vintage. This had been running for three years and was his particular love. It was all mechanically controlled and worked continually day and night. The skins and pips were all spat out from the crusher, and these were fermented and produced a wine which was provided free to the workers. During our visit there was a thunderstorm which cut off the electric supply, but they quickly switched over to their own supply. There were usually two men on

71

duty here, but during the vintage twenty-thirty men occupied sleeping quarters. They reckoned on processing 2500 pipes here during the vintage which lasts about five weeks. I think a pipe measures about one hundred and five gallons.

We had a hair-raising drive back in the thunderstorm over an unmade road alongside the river in the dark, and did not have our meal until 9.30 a.m. after which we were entertained by a neighbouring vintner to coffee and port. It was here we saw the actual treading of the grapes. There were three tanks full of grapes and about eighteen youths treading them with their trousers rolled up above their knees, their arms around each other's shoulders, all singing and accompanied by the ever present Accordionist, who incidentally, got paid more than the pickers, for the latter will not go out to the terraces without him. The actual treading looked most unhygienic, I must say, cigarette ash and all, but it was all great fun and everyone enjoyed themselves immensely. This is a family affair with all the children taking part singing, dancing and feasting, until they literally dropped and went to sleep on the stone floor. We too were shattered, and glad to get to our beds. Everyone was so friendly and welcoming, it was a great experience and one I shall never forget.

PORTUGAL

After breakfast altogether, we said our farewells to our hosts, as they had to leave early to arrange a luncheon for thirty bankers at Regna. We were quite glad to set off on our own again, in a clean car too, as one of the staff had given it a much needed wash. They had all been so kind, and we were more than a little overwhelmed by the hospitality which we had not expected.

We had nothing planned after leaving Sandeman's, but thought we would explore the mountainous country along the Spanish border, it is such magnificent country. The first night was spent at Faundo, at a nice looking Estalogen, the name of which I have forgotten but which which, translated, means "Inn of the Snow." The service, however, was not good, and we lay in bed reading next morning waiting for our breakfast, which did not arrive, tried the telephone, which did not work, so we showered and dressed and went to find someone to give us petit dejeuner, and were glad to be on our way.

It was my birthday, and pouring with rain. We pulled in at Castelo Branco hoping the rain would cease and enable us to walk around, but as there was no hope of this happening, we drove on with the intention of treating ourselves to a nice lunch at Marveo, but still no cheer, so went on through dense woods of Cork trees with oldeander growing wild on the roadside, to Portalegre and here we found a very nice restaurant, where we had stopped four years previously, and then on to Estremoze and booked in at the Pousada da

73

Rainha Santa Isobel. What a contrast it was from the previous night! This was a magnificent castle high on a hill overlooking the town.It was familiar country to us, and I recalled a lovely market place where I had bought a basket on our last visit, and looked forward to seeing it again. We booked in here for two nights. The evening meal was served in a marble banqueting hall, and the "cut off the joint" was from a whole roast lamb brought to the table on a trolley.

We had been told that Marveo was well worth a visit, and indeed this proved to be so-a village built high up in the mountains, within fortified walls overlooking the Spanish border, and we walked around the tiny village on cobbled streets. On leaving, we dropped to the plain and returned to Portalegre, left the car at a garage, and managed, with the help of sign language and a phrase book, to make it understood that we needed the belt to the Alternator adjusted(no mean achievement, we thought), then walked around trying to find a little shop to which Antonio had taken us and where I had purchased a Cork Cooler, but had no luck. We went to Elvas, and this too was well worth visiting, and again a fortified town on the top of a hill, with distinct Moorish influence, and where a huge Aqueduct still stood, built by the Moors, who were driven out in 1226. Dropping to the plains, we passed through the richest agricultural area we had seen so far. The Ranchos looked well organised, with large flocks of sheep, herds of cattle and goats, and flocks of turkeys each with their own drovers and herdsmen, with a dog in attendance, and a vast area under the plough.

We were confined to our room next day, feeling rather frustrated awaiting a call from Tom Huggins of Sandeman's who was going to try and book for us to travel on the Eagle Star sailing on October 11th. We tried telephoning him, but kept contacting somebody who could not speak English, but he eventually came through saying he had been successful.

We explored Elvora, and found it to be a busy city marred by the noise of traffic, but what city isn't? It possessed a beautiful cathedral and lovely old buildings, and we lunched in the cloisters of a convent, after which, we went on to Serpa, and found a Pousada standing alongside a tiny church, situated on a hill surrounded by olive trees and overlooking flat cultivated land with a backdrop of mountains.

We chatted to fellow guests, a couple from Ohio who were en route for Seville. He described himself as "an Enamel Picker" and it took me a little while to realise he was a Dentist!

After breakfast we drove south hoping to find some sunshine, but after an hour's drive ran into a terrific storm. We were stopped by La Guarda for passport inspection at a place near the Spanish border and ran into such a downpour that our speed dropped to 2 mph, and eventually arrived at Monte Gordo, the first town in the Algarve after Spain. We parked the car, and on our return from shopping, were greeted by a lady in the adjacent car saying in a strong Lancashire accent "Ee tha's picked up some muck" and she was right, the car was filthy! En route for Pria de Rocha, we called in at the picturesque fishing village of Portimao. The harbour was packed with colourful sardine boats, the weather obviously being too rough to put to sea. The hotels in the Algarve were very busy, but eventually we found accommodation. The service in the dining room was poor, the hotel being full of Germans on a package tour. We were not lucky with the weather on this trip, but we donned our mackintoshes and walked as far as we could in a westerly direction, but everywhere there were concrete piles being erected. Portimao however was a very pleasant place with plenty to watch in the harbour. The sun actually came out, and we sat at a pavement cafe and watched the world go by. We selected The Penguin for our evening meal, and this turned out to be run by an ex naval couple. The husband seemed to do most of the drinking, and his ex-Wren wife everything else, but they provided a good meal with "vin de Casa" (wine on the house). There was odd company in the dining room, obviously residents, including two old dears (probably my age) sitting at separate tables and carrying on a conversation in very high-class plummy voices, which was all quite amusing.

Next day, Oct 6th we did some shopping in Portimao, then drove to a Pousada in Sagres, where we managed to book the last available room. The weather had improved at last, and after a picnic lunch, we changed into our swim-suits and basked in the sun on the beach. The Cicadas were busy here, reminding us very much of the Cape, and they, together with the fishermen going out to sea, gave us a very disturbed night. We visited Cape St. Vincent again, which we had enjoyed so much last time.

We left the Hotel de Baleria having enjoyed our two days there immensely, and travelled towards Lisbon, along roads banked with Aloes, Bamboo and Carica. On the way we called at Sines on the coast, and arrived at Santiago do Cacem in time for lunch at the Pousada de Sao Tiago where we had been twice before. After studying the official list of Pousadas we decided to give the Hotel Esperdante at Sesimbra a try, not knowing anything about the place. It was a most fortunate choice, and we were given a room with a balcony overlooking the beach, where we had our breakfast next morning. I was up in the night watching the fishermen out in the bay, shining bright lights on the water to attract the fish. "Esperdante", we discovered was Portuguese for the Swordfish, and this, apparently was a renowned centre for the deep sea fishing. There was great excitement when a fisherman landed with his catch – a huge Esperdante, which was weighed and hung from a gallows like structure whilst the fisherman had his photograph taken alongside his catch.

We crossed the magnificent bridge over the Tagus, then

76

endured a nightmare drive in roaring traffic to Lisbon. The Portuguese seem to take no notice of traffic lights or signals, which was all quite horrifying, but, eventually, finding somewhere to park, we walked to Sandeman's office in the city, and there, once again, were treated like royalty. Mariana, the Secretary, provided us with a drink of Clipper, and handed over the tickets for the Eagle ferry which they had acquired for us. I remember the price shook us rather – one hundred and six pounds when we expected them to be about seventy five.

We wanted to visit Cascais again, but found it very busy, and were lucky to find a penthouse suite on the topmost floor of the "Cidadela". The lift took us up five floors, then we had two flights of stairs. The first thing we did was examine the tariff on the back of the door, and found it to be the most expensive room we had had yet. To help alleviate the cost we lunched in our suite, a meal of bread and cheese and a delicious pineapple. Also, instead of going to have my hair dressed, I washed it myself and sat outside in the sun to dry it. Everything seemed very expensive, which was not surprising, after all it was a millionaire's playground, and the place was full off noisy Americans, members of the New Yorks Builders Association and their wives. We retired, but were awakened at 5 a.m. by the hotel header tank warming up and making the most weird noises.

We took a train into Lisbon and strolled around window shopping and sat at a pavement cafe on the Avenue de Liberdardi, which is a most impressive tree lined road, to watch the people, all beautifully dressed, before returning to Cascais. This is where Jonathan and Linda spent their honeymoon in 1971.We found a delightful fish restaurant for lunch, and decided to return there for our evening meal.

Our last drive was to Sintra, on the coast, a strange place with two magnificent palaces. The last day of any holiday can be a bit dreary, and having packed up and left the hotel we didn't know quite what to do with ourselves, so drove slowly along the coast, admiring the summer residences of the wealthy, and after a light lunch arrived at Alcante about 2.15 p.m. and joined the queue of cars waiting to board the ferry, where we had a wait of one and a half hours. Eventually we boarded and found our cabin amidships on C deck. Henry was not feeling very well, so after a light meal we retired to our bunks and slept very well considering the noise of the engines.

The mileage read three thousand and thirty seven miles when we boarded, so we had done quite a bit of driving in one month.

We packed up ready for off on October 13th and spent a tedious morning waiting to dock at Southampton, and were once again in dear old England, and glad to be back.

On arrival at Glebe House at 5 a.m. we found the house lovely and warm, the table set for four, flowers on the table, a tea tray set for two, vegetables ready to cook and a casserole already in the bottom oven of the Aga. What a great welcome! Jonathan and Linda arrived soon after six a.m. and we spent a lovely evening together.

So ended another trip abroad. Where to next I wonder? I am getting quite a taste for travel.

CRETE

I have no record of this holiday, but I know that we were inspired by Pat and Nancy Maguire on meeting them at Dale, who are great enthusiasts of ancient Greece and Greek Mythology.

We booked a Fly-drive holiday through The Heraklion Club for students recommended by Peter and Rita Rennie

We flew from Gatwick for the first time, and to our great surprise, Pat and Nancy were on the same flight. They were with a party and had a pretty tight schedule, but we did manage to have a meal together during our visit.

We collected our car, a Suzuki, which just about accommodated ourselves and luggage.

We visited Knossis and spent a morning wandering around the ruins, and of course there are plenty of ruins to visit in Greece, and we spent a great deal of time ambling through and over them. I must admit I am not a lover of ancient history and ruins, but I did appreciate the lovely country and the people.

The coast road to Rethimnon was beautiful, and lined with oldeander, geraniums and spartis in full bloom. We had no difficulty in booking hotels and everywhere we went we ate in tavernas on the sea front and enjoyed the national dishes.

We decided to visit a doctor as Henry was not well, and called at the tourist Information Office to enquire of one. I recall the little man in charge left a number of would-be enquirers to escort us down the street to a doctor who gave Henry a thorough examination and a prescription for an antibiotic, some syrup and pills for breathlessness.

At a shop a few doors away, we purchased bread, wine and Feta, the local goat cheese, and set off along the coast road once more for Kania, had our picnic by the lovely blue sea, and arrived at Khanis, where, in the port area, we found a hotel with a balcony, as we felt that Henry would benefit from a restful day or two. He was only fit for sleeping and sitting, the effect of the pills chiefly, so this place was ideal, with a lovely view from the balcony, and only a few steps to a choice of tavernas.

Henry was much better the next day, thank goodness, so we shopped for our usual bread and wine, and Henry invested in a pair of very nice ankle boots, which I think, cost about 1600Drs, and which Jonathan still probably possesses. We drove west along the coast, turning off at Kolimbari onto a lovely headland, and after lunch followed a side road that took our fancy, up a mountainside, and discovered a magnificent memorial in concrete, with eleven names inscribed on a marble slab. Not being able to read Greek, we had no idea as to the people remembered, and why. Henry was very keen to visit the war memorial st Souda Bay where a number of his fellow Marines were remembered from the landings in Crete. It was beautifully kept, and we wandered around for some time and picked a few names we knew.

On leaving Hania, we went south to Spakion, a most spectacular drive over mountains and through gorges, and thoroughly enjoyed it. There was a plain with hundred of windmills whirling away obviously supplying power for somewhere or something, but I cannot remember where this was, and we found a country taverna for lunch, where we saw the owner roasting whole tiny lambs, which we ate with our fingers, no implements being provided. They were delicious, but it seemed awfully cruel.

We dropped down to the coast again, stopping at small villages for a drink, and were plied by Greeks sitting at the next table under a tree with their local drink, from the same vessel as they had used. It is bad manners and, they consider, an insult, to refuse, and they all laughed heartily when I pulled a wry face at the taste, and went back to my beer.

Matala had the only sandy beach we had seen, everywhere is so rocky, and this beach was pretty filthy. There were caves in the cliff-side opposite our hotel, which appeared to be occupied by gypsies and yobbos.

It was the month of May when we went, a delightful time to go and before the influx of holiday crowds. I think the ideal way to travel would be with a back pack, and Island hop as the fancy took one.

SINGAPORE and MELBOURNE-1976

We left Glebe House on Wednesday Feb 18th, having left Benjy at the kennels, much to his disgust, he is so reluctant to go which makes us feel such cads. We had packed the car the previous day and set off after breakfast, during which Jonathan called and presented me with a beautiful orchid for my buttonhole. The weather was cold and miserable with a sprinkling of snow lying on the ground, and we were glad to arrive at Ellinor's without mishap, and she drove us to the Airport, where we did not have to wait long before boarding. The flight was delayed three quarters of an hour through engine trouble, but I don't mind how long I have to wait so long as the engines pass all safety tests. So we set off once more on our travels, I am really getting quite blasé about flying. This time I got totally confused with the time alterations – one hour difference at Frankfurt where we spent half an hour, and on leaving at 9.30 p.m. had to alter our watches two hours, and on arrival at Bahrain at five o' clock, a further four hours. We were able to stretch our legs a bit here and left at six, and from then on we could see the terrain over which we were flying – mostly desert, then across India and arrived Bangkok at 4 a.m. where we again altered our watches by half an hour and arrived at Singapore 7.30 p.m. feeling like damp rags, but were surprised and delighted to find Roger and Enid waiting to welcome us. These are old friends of ours who lived opposite to us at Dale. Roger was employed at the Ministry of Works and had had several spells abroad, this time doing a clearing-up job in Singapore. They drove us to our hotel where we enjoyed a drink and a chat about old times together, and left us after making plans to meet again. We felt a little better after a bath and a change, a stroll along the road to get the feel of Singapore and a light meal, after which we fell into bed.

Next day we started walking to the Quay, but it was so hot and humid we took a taxi, it really is too hot to do much walking, and after a visit to the bank we taxied back to the hotel where we entertained Enid to lunch. The Quay was most attractive with a huge model of a Merlion (half lion half Fish) at the mouth of the Singapore river, the banks lined with eating stalls, the harbour busy with rice barges travelling along in processions of two or three being towed by the mechanised barge, and everywhere so clean.As we were leaving for Enid's house after lunch a huge bunch of orchids arrived from Rosemary and Betty Newman, with an invitation to a meal with them on Saturday. Betty, a friend of ours from Usk, was on a visit to her daughter Rosemary, whose husband is a Banker, and has been resident in Singapore for about two years.

We got to Adam Drive, Roger and Enid's bungalow, and sat on the verandah enjoying the peace and quiet and listening to the liquid song of a Golden Oriole. The garden was lovely with hibiscus and oldeander in full bloom, the bungalow, a long low three bedroomed building, in a bit of a muddle at the moment as they were in the throes of packing up in preparation to leaving for the U.K. On Roger's return home from work, we all took the dog Pero for a walk. We walked past a small Chinese Campon which seemed to be swarming with children who all stopped playing to stare at us as objects of great interest, then up a rise to the golf course, passing two elaborate chinese graves by the roadside.

As Roger and Enid were so occupied with packing up, we thought it a good idea to spend a few days visiting

Penang, but the travel agents informed us there were no bookings available. Roger and Enid insisted on us staying with them, and they collected us and our luggage, saw us installed in their lovely bungalow, left us to make ourselves a sandwich lunch, and took themselves off for a game of golf. We went for a walk in the Botanical gardens later, which were a wealth of colour and beautifully laid out, then Roger drove us to Rosemary's truly magnificent bungalow. Her husband is in banking, and they have a cook, and a nanny for their small son. We spent a most enjoyable evening with them, and had a sumptuous meal – notable for my introduction to avocado, to which I have become addicted.

We had a lovely day out with Roger and Enid on the Sunday, they took us to the Malaya peninsula, where we had a lunch of prawns in a fishing village named Kikup. The houses were tiny wooden shacks built on stilts over the water, all connected by walkways made from planks of wood. Walking over these was quite a feat, and the cheery little children took great delight in jumping into the filthy water as we passed and drenching us, as they shrieked with delight. There was a strong smell of fish everywhere, the catches being hung out on lines in the sun to dry. The fish restaurant was quite an experience too, here we sat at a table with an oilcloth covering, a huge dish of prawns put in the centre of the table, fingers were used and the shells discarded over the rail adding to the debris in the sea. The toilet facilities consisted of a hole in the floor through which one could see the sea-not very hygienic.

The air conditioning in the bungalow at Adam Drive, was a large ceiling fan, and Enid gave us Mosquito coils to burn overnight, and advised us to leave our clothes well away from the windows, all of which had fancy wrought iron on the outside to deter thieves. On one occasion Roger had had his trousers removed from a chair by means of a pole with a hook on the end inserted through the window, he found them on the garden path next morning with empty pockets.

An early start is made to work in the morning, and Roger leaves the house at 7.30 a.m. There is a time restriction on cars in the city and no car is allowed to enter after this has been put into force unless one has a pass. Enid took us to Holland Park shopping centre, where we bought Batik shirts, a skirt, and I placed an order for a dress to be made – full length, sleeveless, with a mandarin collar, in a lovely blue and gold pattern, to be ready in twenty four hours. Henry visited a shoe shop, and the Chinese owner went to a lot of trouble, but Henry was not suited, and on rising, or attempting to, found he was fixed to the seat by a broken spring which penetrated his trousers. I was not in the shop at the time, but Henry gave a hilarious account of him leaning over whilst the Chinaman endeavoured to extract the spring.

We had to visit the famous Raffles of course, where we had sandwiches and beer in a lofty room which had an air of faded Edwardian splendour, then went for a walk along the waterfront, which is so interesting with all the hustle and bustle, noise and smells, the latter very plentiful. The Lighters were alongside the wharf being unloaded, and the barges with their cargo of rice trailing two, sometimes three rafts behind them. The food stalls along the wharf are busy all the time, the cooking being done on burners in Woks, and the customers sitting on benches or standing with their bowls of prawns and rice and chicken, stuffing the food into their mouths with chopsticks with amazing dexterity. I loved it all. We took a taxi home, ready for a cup of tea and a cool off, and just made it before a terrific storm broke. The storms are of short duration and rain comes down in great sheets – filling the monsoon ditches which are large enough to take a Mini and line each side of the road – in no time at all, and then it is all over, the streets steaming, and the ditches empty. After supper Roger took us to see a Chinese Opera. These take place in a street on an open-air stage which was brilliantly lit, and the performers brightly dressed and heavily made up. The audience sit around on a few chairs, some bring their own, but most stand, and the children clamber onto the stage. There is a great deal of noisy sound effects off stage, banging of gongs etc. Apparently this continues for ten hours or so with the audience coming and going, and the opera is well known by all and performed annually. This all takes place in the midst of high rise flats which house thousands of Chinese and Malays, the population of Singapore being two and one quarter million and the island is only twenty by eighteen square miles. The flats, we were told, only have two rooms both of which are bedrooms, the eating is all done at the stalls outside, and the washing hung from windows and balconies.

We took a taxi to Jerong Bird Park and spent about four hours there. This is situated in a natural valley and is beautifully planned, and has the highest man-made waterfall. All the area is covered with netting reaching a great height, and birds of all species and colour fly around freely. Another storm broke as we left the park, and we were glad of the umbrellas Enid insisted on us buying on our first shopping expedition, and were literally paddling across the road to a bus stop. Friends joined us for a curry meal in the evening – Tom and Connie Chatterton, he was in charge of the war graves in the area.

Packing started in earnest for us all as we were leaving for a hotel, The Equatorial, and the official packers were collecting Enid and Roger's goods and chattels to store into containers ready for the voyage home. Henry and I left them hard at it and went to Holland Park to collect the dress I had had made, for which I paid the sum of seven pounds and which I still have, although goodness knows when I shall wear it, it looks rather like a fancy dress here, but I am reluctant to part with it, it conjures up happy memories. We took our friends out for a meal at The Troica, and had a most enjoyable evening, finishing with a drink and a chat before retiring, we seemed to do a great deal of talking! Henry finished a painting he was doing from the verandah, and presented it to Enid, as a souvenir of our visit.

We were all up early next day, and after breakfasting together, we decided we would be better out of the way, and took a taxi to our hotel. After confirming our flight to Hongkong for Sat 28th, we went to the bank to equip ourselves with Hongkong dollars, then made our way to Mount Faber where we boarded a cable car to the Island of Santosa, and a very hair-raising trip it was as we left terra firma, but interesting to look down on the Chinese Campons, and over the water so busy with river traffic. It was so hot, we decided to have a meal first, then went to visit the scene of the signing of the Peace Pact, depicted in life size wax figures displayed in huge glass cases – air conditioned of course – then on to an exhibition of Gunners, which was of no interest to me, but fascinated Henry, and a Coralarium – a beautiful display of coral and fish and left the island by boat for Singapore. We were not very impressed with Santosa, which is a development specially for the tourist having a roller skating rink, a golf course, many chalets, and a great deal more in the pipeline. We were glad to get back to the hotel and enjoy a wallow in a bath, and after changing, met Enid and Roger in the foyer and they took us to Tom and Connie's for a meal of Beef Fondue followed by fresh peaches and cream. Poor Enid was so tired, and the packers have not yet finished at Adam Drive.

We planned a lazy day, and spent most of it in and out of the hotel swimming pool, after which Enid and Roger joined us for a meal – a typical Chinese meal with all the dishes, in the centre of the table – bowls of rice of course, chicken in a sauce, pork in a sauce, shrimps etc. I managed chopsticks quite well I thought, for the first attempt.

This was the last we saw of our friends for some time,

they have been so kind and welcoming, despite the difficulties they had to cope with, packing everything up to go back to England, and we have had such a happy time together.

There is one interesting item I forgot to mention earlier – all young men have to have short hair, and there are notices in the Post Office saying any with shoulder length hair are to go back to the end of the queue, they were checked at the Airport too.

Farewell Singapore, we have enjoyed the visit so much. It is a delightful place, how horrifying it must have been when overrun by the Japanese.

HONGKONG

We flew in a Tristar with the plane fully loaded, had excellent service and free drinks during what was called "The Happy Hour", and arrived on time but had to wait an hour for our baggage. We got to the hotel about 5 p.m. feeling very tired, and retired early with the intention of exploring next day. We arose refreshed and ready for anything the day might bring.

I was amazed at the immensely tall buildings and high-rise flats all crammed together, the chatter and the bustle, the wonderful chaos of stalls, rickshaws and bicycles, with everything and everybody moving at such a speed. We decided the best thing to do would be to take a four hour tour to Kowloon and the New Territories, and found this very interesting, including the sordid area of Aberdeen Harbour, of which, more later, as well as the lovely coastline as we climbed a hill overlooking the Chinese border. We were not allowed, at that time, to cross the border, only permitted to gaze across the expanse, and have our thoughts on Chairman Mao!

To take a tour is the only way to get the feel of a city when time is so limited. There is so much to see here, and we wished we had more time, maybe we shall come again one day.

We arrived back at the hotel in nice time to have a bath and change, then walked to the Hongkong Hotel, where we had a fabulous meal of marinated Trout, Lamb Cutlets cooked over charcoal, baked Potato and salad, wine and coffee, all beautifully served. Walking back along the waterfront, we stood and admired all the illuminations, the large floating restaurants in the harbour, the numerous boats with their lights twinkling, all reflected in the water, and the streets ablaze with electric signs advertising everything under the sun, including topless barmaids, and everywhere so crowded.

After lunch next day, we went on an Island tour by coach passing through an undersea tunnel, which was completed in 1972, to a vehicular car which took us up 1820 feet to overlook Hongkong harbour, but it was cold and misty, and we were glad to board the coach again. Altogether, it was a disappointing day weather-wise, cold dull and dreary, and every time we stopped we were accosted by pedlars and touts. We visited the Tiger gardens, which, in our opinion, were an abomination, containing huge plastic gaudily painted figures, built by a millionaire with a quirky mind. We had seen much of what we disliked, and felt we needed pampering, and indeed, we had this treatment when we went to The Baron's Table for a meal, recommended by the Kuoni agent's wife, beautifully served in authentic surroundings.

Neither of us felt very bright next day, but enjoyed strolling round window shopping, and after a sandwich lunch, took a ferry to the Island and explored the ladder street area – a street of steps lined with beggars and traders accompanied by plenty of noise and smells. We were pretty exhausted after this and decided to stay in the hotel for a meal that evening.

The sun shone for the first time during our visit, so we boarded a boat for a cruise round the Harbour next afternoon, which proved to be a very interesting tour.

The harbour traffic is ceaseless, and the people living on board their little boats are a race on their own, who seldom go ashore, and marry their own kind. All the boats appeared to have numerous children and dogs on board. The Walla Wallas and the Junks in the Typhoon Basin were a sight to see, the boats crammed together with narrow planks connecting one to another. The smells were horrific, and we were glad to return to a hot bath.

That evening we went to the Hongkong Hotel again, but this time to the sixth floor. The Canberra was in harbour, and looked so near one felt one could reach out and touch it. It was not until we returned home that we learnt that Henry's cousin Vera and her husband were on board enjoying a world cruise. What a pity! We would have enjoyed seeing them. The illuminated boats in the harbour, and the Canberra all lit up, made a lovely sight. I must say all the meals we had in Hongkong were superb, and that night we actually danced on a tiny dance floor in the restaurant, and walked back to our hotel replete and happy, and did some packing before retiring.

I visited the hairdresser next morning, at an exorbitant cost, we settled the hotel bill and took a taxi to the airport. It is a pity the weather was so cold and windy, and consequently we were not sorry to be leaving for warmer climes, nevertheless, we found Hongkong exciting, and knew there was so much more to see, our short stay was nothing like enough.

On board the Boeing 707, we put our watches back one hour, had a late lunch, and arrived in Bangkok about 5 p.m.

It amazes me how easily one can pop from one country to another, and see such different ways of life.

BANGKOK

We were greeted by the Kuoni agent, and were delighted to find a letter from Ellinor. We did not plan to do anything until the morrow, when we hoped we would be fresher.

The first impressions of Bangkok were of happy smiling people, uneven pavements, and dust and dirt everywhere, very prominent after the cleanliness of Singapore. We were told later however, that the city had been flooded to the depth of one foot at the end of the rainy season, which would account for a lot of the untidiness.

The tour of the Royal Palace and the Temple of the Emerald Buddha, which we took after lunch, is difficult to describe, it is all so ornate and fantastic.

We removed our shoes on entering the temple, and sat crossed-legged on the floor with our guide, who explained a little about Buddhism, and although he was Catholic, nintey per cent are Buddhist. There was an extravagant use of gold leaf everywhere. Later he took us to a Lapidary where we saw fabulous stones being cut and set, and although they tried hard to sell us a Ruby Eternity ring, we could not afford the fifty pounds asked, and emerged ringless.

We retired early as the thought of being called at 5.30 next day appalled us. Actually it was not too bad getting up so early, and off we went on the River tour, but were tired on returning to the hotel at 11.45 a.m.

The river market used to be in the city centre, but there are now so many river taxis tearing around on the water at high speed like Hell's Angels, and creating such a wash, that the traders in their sampans loaded with goods, have difficulty in keeping afloat, consequently the market had to move up river. It was a very picturesque scene. Some sampans loaded with fruit and vegetables, some with bread, some had a cooker on board and were serving hot dishes, and some were plying fresh drinking water, all jostling for a position nearest the prospective buyer, and it was all so colourful, the girls in brightly coloured cottons, and all wearing straw hats hiding their smiling faces.

We arrived back at the hotel, very hot tired and dirty. We found the noise, and the pollution quite exhausting in the heat, and slept soundly for an hour after lunch. Later we walked down Wireless Road to a jeweller which the Kuoni agent had recommended, where Henry bought me a Ruby ring to celebrate our Ruby wedding the following year, and some bracelets and jewellery to take home as gifts.

In the evening we decided to try a Thai restaurant, which was interesting, and on pleading ignorance of the dishes to the head waiter, and explaining that we did not wish to have anything too spicy, he helped us to choose – a bowl of rice each, a dish of diced pork, one of beef and onion in a hot sauce, and grilled lobster, followed by a dish of prepared fresh fruits – papaya, pineapple and melon, all of which we enjoyed enormously, sitting at a table under a pagoda covered with hibiscus. We had to barter for a taxi to the hotel, and a very hair-raising drive it was too.

After all this excitement, we decided Sunday would really be a day of rest, and we spent a lovely day in and out of the hotel pool, sleeping and eating in the heat of the sun.

We joined a party visiting the City temples, which are everywhere, and so ornate with their golden pinnacles, and tiny golden bells hanging outside tinkling in the occasional waft of air. We were introduced to the reclining Buddha, an immense figure, and the sitting Buddha of pure gold. This was purchased by a man in memory of his mother, in what he thought was stone, being all that he could afford, but during the removal from one site to another, it was dropped and cracked open to reveal a solid gold figure, so Mum did rather well, or rather son did! We stopped only to have a welcome drink of coconut milk from the shell. In the afternoon we walked to the County store and shopped for Thai silk, but it was really too hot for walking, and the pavements were dirty, dusty and uneven, and we were glad to return to the hotel and cool off in the pool. That evening we joined a party at a Thai restaurant, where we sat on the floor and watched a display of Thai dancing. The girls are so beautiful, each movement so graceful and expressive, long nails attached to each finger, their feet used too, with every muscle and joint perfectly controlled

We were out for the whole day next day, leaving the hotel at 0700 and drove one hundred and ten kms through agricultural land and rice paddies, stopping en route to see people making salt. The water was left in huge pools to dry out in the sun, and the residue collected when all moisture had evaporated, then transported in pans borne on the heads of the women labourers.

On arrival at the river we boarded a water taxi, which took us at great speed (a la James Bond) to the floating market. On going ashore we were immediately pestered by traders, but warned by our guide not to purchase anything until our return to the boat. I did a bit of bargaining, at which I got quite efficient, and bought a Batik skirt for myself for fifty Bart after being asked one hundred and fifty Bart. On board again, we were taken through side channels to see how the people lived, mostly in wooden huts with balconies over the water, which looked filthy. Some maidens were submerged in it and washing their hair – we thought they were wasting their time!

We drew alongside a floating bar on which we climbed, and were given a very refreshing fruit punch, and were then towed quietly and peacefully along the main river to the Rose Garden floating restaurant for lunch. We enjoyed wandering through the beautifully laid out gardens, so full of exotic plants and bright with colour, then visited a Thai village and watched craftsmen and women at work. We saw Thai silk being made, and were introduced to the mysteries of Batik printing. We then entered an arena with benches arranged in tiers on three sides, and watched a display of various dances each depicting a story, a procession escorting a monk to his initiation ceremony, Thai Boxing (which looked highly dangerous), Cock fighting, Stick fighting, a wedding ceremony, a Thai ball game, and lastly outside, watched elephants at work transporting huge tree trunks from one bank of the lake to another;all most enjoyable and interesting. We were then directed to the "Happy House" which proved to be the toilet.

For our last meal in Thailand, we chose to go to the Chit Pochona which was good, but unfortunately Henry had some beer spilt down his trousers. The head waiter was most concerned, and we found that eight bart had been deducted from our bill!

After breakfast on Wednesday March 10th, we settled our hotel bill, purchased a silk tie for Henry, took a taxi to the airport, and boarded a Boeing 707 for the easy flight to Singapore, where we arrived in a thunderstorm.

The taxi drove us through streets awash to our hotel. We telephoned Roger and Enid to make arrangements to meet up for the last time, and had a pleasant evening with them at Gino's, said our farewells, and arranged to meet again in Dale at the Easter Hooley. By then, they would be settled once again in their house in Castle Way.

We discovered "Chain Alley" next day, a narrow alley packed with open stalls with room for only two to walk abreast, and the vendors doing their best to sell their wares. There were stalls of spices, brightly coloured clothing alongside food and crafts of every description. A wonderful place, but, sadly I learn it is non existent today.

We packed and said goodbye to Singapore – a visit we have enjoyed enormously.

—————————— C୫ୠଠ ——————————

MELBOURNE and SYDNEY

After boarding the plane, we were informed of an engine fault, and the Captain wished to test it on the runway before take-off. He did not like the result and took us back to the terminal, where we sat around until 2 a.m. without being told anything. Then we were told to go to gate 8 only to find that we were being taken to a hotel for the night, with no luggage, which was all aboard the plane. It was a most frustrating time. We were captive in the hotel until 7 p.m. the next day, and tempers were running high. Singapore airport was in utter chaos, and no one appeared to know what was happening. At last we succeeded in getting tickets and boarding passes on a London-Sydney-Melbourne plane, but this plane again was delayed by a fault, and we took off at 11 p.m. very hungry, tired and frustrated. We were given free drinks on board, and all lodged bitter complaints about lack of co-operation, but agreed it was wholly desirable to have the engines in perfect order, but would have been happier had we been informed of what was happening.

We were relieved to arrive at Melbourne, and so pleased to see John Birrell waiting for us. He drove us to his home in Toorak, where we received a terrific welcome from Jo, Sara and the dogs. It was about eighteen months since Jo and Sara had visited us at Glebe House, they were with us for only two days, and I recall we tore around the countryside showing them as much as possible. John and Jo were entertaining friends that evening, nine in all, one being the brother-in-law of Booth, who owns many book shops in Hay-on Wye.

Our hosts took us to see the penguin Reserve on Philip Island, about one and one half hours run from Melbourne. We sat on benches alongside a fenced off area, which was dotted with hundreds of burrows, and waited for darkness to fall. As the daylight faded, we could hear rustling and squeaks from the burrows, and saw a small head pop out here and there. We waited spellbound and in absolute silence, and were rewarded by the sight of small penguins popping out of the breakers, shaking themselves, and waddling up the beach in pairs to the rookery and their own particular burrow to feed their young by regurgitation. At first there were about thirty then the numbers grew and grew with the same sudden explosion from the sea, and we watched hundreds of them. These are the fairy penguins, only found in Australia and N. Zealand, and the only ones to live in burrows, which are three – four feet deep. It was a fascinating sight.

We had hoped to visit the Great Barrier Reef and stay on Heron Island, but on visiting an agent, we were disappointed to find we could not afford it as we were restricted as to the amount of currency we were allowed to take with us in those days. We set about planning a trip to the Snowy Mountains instead.

In the meantime we renewed our acquaintance with Norman Wilson, who had stayed with us at Island House, and was a director of Fibremakers, and spent a pleasant evening with him, his wife Dorothy, John and Jo, at a restaurant where I was introduced to Oysters for the first time, and enjoyed them thoroughly. The Wilsons have a ranch outside Melbourne, which we hope to visit before we leave the country.

Jo took us to an animal sanctuary where we viewed emu, looking very moth-eaten and dejected, kangaroo in different sizes, the largest looking terrifyingly powerful; wallaby, and that strange mammal, the Platypus.

John and Jo went out to a previous engagement, and left

Sara to cook us a meal and after we had retired she came knocking on our door to tell us the news that Harold Wilson had stepped down.

After breakfast, Henry and I went into the city by train and visited the New Zealand Tourist board, Cooks, and British Airways, and later Fibremakers city office, where we met their travel man Ron George, who was most helpful and arranged a car for us. We planned to drive to Aldebury, Snowy Mountains, Canberra, and on to Sydney to spend three days with Grenville, our nephew, before returning to Melbourne via the coast road. Before setting off on this expedition, however, the four of us spent a day with the Wilsons on their ranch in Kerrie, about fifty miles out of Melbourne.

The ranch covered one thousand acres, they had seven magnificent Hereford bulls, and we drove round after lunch to see if any new calves had been dropped by the cows, and found ten healthy animals. We met the manager and the Jackaroo (apprentice), saw flocks of brightly coloured eagle, white cockatoos, and kookaburra emitting their strange laughing call. It was a most enjoyable day and so interesting to see life on a real Australian ranch. On the way home, it was quite a sight to see the barbeques on the banks of the river Yarrow all busy. These are built by the council and fired by gas, for which one has to put a coin in a slot.

I went to the market with Jo, I always enjoy them, and it was interesting to see the wide variety of fruit and vegetables, and after a snack lunch we went to see La Trobe's Cottage. La Trobe was the first Governor of New South Wales. We went on to see the Music Bowl donated by Myers, the big store owners, and The Shrine, a memorial to the fallen in the first world war – a dreadfully ugly building I thought, on a beautiful site. That evening John took us to Frenchy's for a meal, apparently the place to go in Melbourne. I did not enjoy it very much, it was too dark and noisy, and I was too tired.

Henry collected a very nice new Escort for our trip, and we set off in high spirits, quite glad to be on our own again, although John and Jo are so kind and we enjoy being with them immensely. Henry had been to the Snowy Mountains before, and he was eager to show me everything. We did about one hundred and fifty miles on the first day, and managed to get accommodation in a second class Motel. Motels provide most of the accommodation in Australia, and none have restaurants, but most provide breakfast. We strolled down the road to a Wimpey and had ham-steaks and chips, and walking back to our little cabin, we picked out the Southern Cross shining brightly in the sky.

We set off early – about 8 a.m. with me at the wheel. I found it a very easy car to drive, and very comfortable. It was a Sunday, and most petrol stations were closed, however, we found one which obligingly opened up for us at Tallangatta, and followed the Murray river valley to Corryong. Most of the road was unsurfaced, but the river was beautiful with weeping willows along the banks, and we stopped whenever we felt like it to admire the beauty.

There were flocks of brightly coloured eagle flying around, and the radiator grille collected masses of large grasshoppers with yellow bodies and red wings.

We crossed the river at Khancoban and started climbing. The scenery was magnificent, and we stopped at Scammells Spur look-out for a picnic, then climbed to 5100 feet to Dead Horse Gap, and reached Thredbo village. This very picturesque village is a skiing centre in the season, with three chair lifts. We stayed at The Lake Motel on Lake Jindabyne, and had a lovely room overlooking the water. I love the place names, they seem to roll off the tongue. We called at the Information Centre at Sawpit Creek in the National Park to gain knowledge of the area, and following the summit road, we came to an unsealed surface, parked the car and followed a forest trail for about two hours, but were disappointed not to see any animals. We returned to

Jindabyne and enjoyed a nice cool beer, and later took the road out to Eucumbene, enjoying the scenic beauty and walking across the dams, then back to our motel with a flock of white and yellow cockatoos flying overhead.

The Snowy Mountain Hydro-Electric Scheme, is a wonderful achievement. Its object is to direct water previously flowing east, inland for irrigation and electricity generation, done by erecting a series of dams and power stations, all in the Kosciuscko National Park. Needless to say the Eucalyptus is everywhere. There are many varieties, but the common blue was here in profusion, and in the heat of the sun one can smell the oil, which causes terrific explosions in the dreaded forest fires.

The Snowgum predominates other growth above fifteen hundred metres, but the alpine area, above nineteen hundred metres is quite treeless, but here, lovely alpine plants grow. Birds galore are seen in the lower wooded area – the crimson rosell, the white cockatoo, and the kookaburra.

We visited Kianda before making our way to Canberra, which was the scene of a gigantic but short lived gold rush in 1860, with the gold being panned at Pollocks Creek, a small stream winding through a high altitude plain. It was hard to imagine ten thousand men living here in shacks and tents, all panning for gold; one hundred and seventy thousand ounces being uncovered altogether. It was all worked out in twelve months, and in 1862 there were only two hunded and fifty people there. Now all that one sees is a couple of broken down shacks, a few gravestones, and heaps of stones everywhere, and it is left to the imagination to picture what life must have been like.

We retraced our steps and visited the new town of Adaminaby, the old one being submerged in a man made lake, with skeleton trees protruding from the water. We followed a gravel road for forty one miles across country, up and over the mountain range, a tortuous journey which took us two and one half hours, and it was a relief to get onto tarmac and to drive the fifteen miles to Canberra in comfort.

Our first impression of the capital, was of a clean, well planned city, and we looked forward to exploring it. We found it quite difficult at first to find our way around, but it was easy once we realised it was all planned in circuits, about four outer ones, then the State circle and Capital Hill.

It was all beautifully planned with wide roads planted with trees, and not one building an eyesore. All of this had been built since Henry first visited it. We went first to the War Memorial, and spent much time viewing the various rooms displaying war episodes, but the Pool of Reflection was the most impressive Hall of Memory I had ever been in. After driving round the city, we parked the car and took a cruise on the man-made lake and viewed everything from the water. Unfortunately, we missed the Carillon which rings only at given times. The Carillon has fifty-three bells, the largest in the world, and was presented by Britain to commemorate the golden jubilee of the National Capital of Australia, and it was interesting to learn that the wood used in the manufacture of the clavier, came from a century old oak beam which was removed from Taylor's factory, Loughborough, who have been casting bells for centuries.

We left Canberra for Sydney next day, Henry driving, passing the Embassies, all beautiful buildings built in the style of their respective countries. At Gouldburn about sixty miles from Canberra, we ran into rain, and it really pelted down, and we had a dreary drive along the Hume Highway with many roadworks, and lorries belting along. It was so wet we had to stay in the car for our picnic.

Sydney was a confused mass of traffic, but we managed to

find the hotel Grenville had booked for us (we discovered later that it was in the red light area). We phoned Grenville, and arranged to meet him at The Chevron for a drink, and were slightly surprised to find he was accompanied by a girl friend. Why, I really do not know, for he could never live without one. Jennie was a charming girl, and very much in love with him. They married later, but Jennie, sadly died of cancer a few months after giving birth to a daughter – Phillippa.They took us for a meal at Eliza's, and we spent a most enjoyable evening together. It was good to see Grenville again, and he seemed genuinely delighted to see us.

Henry and I explored the waterfront armed with mackintoshes, strolled outside the famous Opera House, entered, and had coffee overlooking the water and the famous bridge. At the Ferry terminal, we found a harbour cruise was due to leave, which included lunch, so we boarded the boat, and enjoyed seeing famous landmarks from the water, and having a cold lunch and beer. The weather was kind to us too. On landing we walked through The Rocks, the original Sydney seafront, and visited Cadman's Cottage, Sydney's oldest dwelling. This was built one hundred and fifty years ago as a barracks for the Coxswains and crews of the government's boats. Its longest resident was the emancipated convict, John Cadman, who was arrested in 1798 for stealing a horse in the west of England. For this, he was originally sentenced to death, but later this was commuted to "transportation beyond the seas for life". Having lived in the colony for thirty two years, at the age of sixty he married one Elizabeth Mortimer, who, with her two daughters Elizabeth and Charlotte, were transported in 1828, for stealing a hairbrush! They lived for the next fifteen years in the cottage overlooking Sydney Cove, the area now known as The Rocks, he working as a Superintendent of government boats, caulking timbers, mending sails etc. It must have been an exciting place to live in those days, seeing the tall masted Clippers, and to witness the arrival of the first Steam Packet, and the building of the semicircular Quay.

He retired in 1845, bought the lease of The Steam Packet in George St, but died two years later having served the colony well. The cottage fell into disrepair, and it was not until 1971, when The Rocks area was redeveloped, that it was restored.

A barbecue with Grenville and Jenny

We walked along the pedestrian way on the famous bridge and watched motorists throwing their toll fees into huge canvases. On returning to our hotel I treated myself to a Vibromassage on the bed, for which I had to insert 20c in a slot. Grenville and Jennie took us to dine at the rotating restaurant from which we had a wonderful view of Sydney. They arranged to take us for a barbecue on the Saturday, neither of us were very enthusiastic, it not being our favourite way of eating. However, Grenville collected us and took us to their flat, and on to a picnic spot in a wood overlooking the Hawkesbury river at Beuken Bay, and it was a lovely sight to see hundreds of yachts and dinghies taking part in the Saturday Regatta, representing many clubs. I was thrilled to see a Koala nibbling away in the gum tree above us, they are not easy to find in the wild apparently. We found a vacant barbecue, and Grenville got a fire going whilst Jennie and I collected wood of which there was plenty. We jibbed at the size of the steaks, and suggested that we shared one, so they had one and one half each, together with "snags" – salad, cheese and fruit – washed down by a pleasant wine. They really did us proud, but oh! what tremendous eaters the Australians are. I still had difficulty in eating my steak, and surreptitiously fed the kookaburra who came down to eat the scraps. We drove back to the flat, enjoyed a cup of tea, and said our farewells, returning to the hotel feeling tired and too full of food to contemplate doing any more for the rest of the day.

We drove south keeping to the coast through pleasant country not unlike our own South Wales, calling at Bateman's Bay where we saw numerous oyster beds, the speciality in these parts, and where we stayed the night, and on to Merimbula to the South Seas Motel, which had been recommended, but which we found disappointing. We had a meal at the R.S.L., where we had to sign a visitors book before being allowed entrance. We had, of course, heard of the poker machines they have in these clubs, but were quite unprepared for the sight which met our eyes. The large room was lined with them, all being busily played, and the clatter was quite deafening.

We were not sorry to leave Merimbula, and made for Mallacootta which had a population of five hundred, but at Christmas, we were told, this rises to twelve thousand. The surrounding country was beautiful, but the villages and townships seemed to lack character. We found a lovely deserted beach where we sunbathed, walked and even bathed in the Tasman sea. The restaurants were predominately fish specialists, and we dined off a delicious

Lobster Thermidor. On chatting to the barman I expressed my disappointment at the lack of Kangaroos, which I had expected to see everywhere, and he advised us to get up early and visit the golf course, where, he reckoned, we would see "Roos galore". This we did, and on fairways five and six we saw about eight at close quarters, in fact Henry had quite a conversation with one who waggled his ears just like Benjy does when talking to him.

Our next stop was Lakes Entrance, a series of inland lakes with narrow channels to the sea, and her we watched the Scallop fishers coming in with their catch. They were allowed to bring in twenty bags a day, for which they got twenty dollars per bag. On returning to the car, we found we had locked the keys inside, but Henry managed to release a door lock through the window with a bent coat-hanger. We contacted Sara in Melbourne, to say we expected to be back about 4 p.m. next day.

It was April lst, but nothing untoward happened, Henry took the wheel and drove at a gentle pace along the Princes Highway, and arrived ten minutes after Jo, who had been to a meeting, and five minutes before Sara, and received a terrific welcome from Coco and Pom, the poodles. We had got so hot in the car, which had no air conditioning, we were glad to plunge into their swimming pool, and enjoyed reading a letter from Hugh and Liz full of news from home.

We returned the car to Avis in the city, and arranged our flight home for April 10th.

The four of us left next morning, for a trip round the coast south of Melbourne, first to Geelong, where Prince Charles attended the school for a time, then through pleasant seaside resorts, stopping to watch fantastic surf-riders at Torquay, then on to Lorne, Apollo Bay, and across the headland to Port Campbell. Here the sandstone coast was eroded into weird and wonderful sculptured shapes by the great Pacific rollers. We stayed the night at Peterborough Motel, where the landlord, we learnt, was a "Pommie" from

Sussex. There were ten guests, and we sat at a trestle table for our meal, everyone being very chummy. One family from Adelaide were on their way to Portland to collect a puppy, and another were on a touring holiday.

I insisted on panning for gold

There is not much to tell of the next day's travel, which was rather dull driving, but the following day provided a dramatic drive through the Grampions, with rugged peaks, and the lower regions covered in dense forest, and we stopped at Ballarat. Here, at Sovereign Hill, a gold mining site has been preserved exactly as it was when panning first started, with original shops and everyone in costume of the day, with horses and wagons for transport, and tents for dwellings. I insisted on trying my hand at panning, and to enable me to do so, I first had to purchase a licence for the sum of two pounds which permitted me "to mine or dig for gold, reside at, or carry on, or follow any trade or calling, except that of Storekeeper, on such lands within the Colony of Victoria as shall belong to me for these purposes. This License to be in force for 3 months" I still have the Licence and the tiny flecks of gold which are only visible when the

111

small phial in which they lie is shaken vigorously.

Ricky Barratt, son of our friends Ruth and John of Dale, and his wife Eva who had moved to a new house at Hurstbridge outside Melbourne, called for us one day to have lunch with them. Ricky was a pilot for the Ansett line. It was a very new house, and they were in the throes of building a swimming pool. As we were preparing to leave, we spotted about sixteen huge Kangaroos on the hillside across the valley. They are a real menace to the farmers, being so destructive. Galahs were flying around in abundance, and the beautiful Rosalia parrots too. I was not very happy with this visit, as there seemed to be an atmosphere, and on our return to the U.K. Ruth said there was to be a divorce. Ricky has since remarried, left the Ansett line, and is now living in Beirut, giving flying instruction I believe.

I visited the After-Care unit with Jo in which she takes an interest, whilst John and Henry went to the Australian Club, and after a light lunch we called for Jo's mother, who was eighty three and lived in a flat on her own, and we had a pleasant drive to Mount Martha in Port Philip bay where they had spent many holidays in earlier days. It was only an hours run from Melbourne, and Jo's mother enjoyed reminiscing.

After breakfast next day, Henry and I visited "Como", a fine example of an early settlement house, run by the National Trust, and furnished in the original style of the 18th century. We then had our last walk along the banks of the river Yarrow, and on our return concentrated on packing, for we were due to fly out the following day. John and Jo took us to the Airport on Friday April 9th, and we were sad to say goodbye – they have been so kind and given us a most memorable time.

We had been away from home for six weeks, and looked forward to seeing the family and to settling down again at Glebe House with Benjy.

KENYAN SAFARI 1977

We set off from Glebe House on Sunday February 13th having left Benjy at the kennels looking very hurt, he hates to see us leaving. We always plan our holidays Jan-Feb if possible, to avoid some of the awful cold weather, and make for warmer climes.

This was my first visit to Kenya, and I was looking forward to it immensely, having read all the books I could get hold of from the library. Henry had told me about it, he having called en route on a business trip before Independence during the aftermath of Mau-Mau.

Our transport through Mangrove swamps to Robinson Island

We arrived at Smiths Cottage to find Peter and his friend Derek very busy trimming beams of oak from the Royal forest for the house, and after a lovely meal with them, Ellinor drove us to Heathrow, and we left our car with them.

The plane left on time and we had a good flight, albeit a sleepless one, and after witnessing the spectacular African dawn, landed at 0900. It was quite incredible to feel the heat surging in as soon as the plane doors were opened, and on descending the steps one enters a completely different world.

We were taken to the Panafric Hotel, one which we were to visit quite often in the future, got our bearings in the hotel, then met our Safari companions – a middle aged couple Ann and Bill Priestland from Surrey, Sarah Wilkinson, a plump jolly girl of twenty eight, and Peta her friend, a slim dark pretty girl about the same age, who worked in London, and the fifth was a Belgian by the name of Raymon, who was rather shy.

We were only allowed to take the bare necessities on Safari, and it took us some time to sort out what to take and what to leave locked up in the hotel. After breakfast next day, we met our Guide and driver, a Kikuyu named Geoffrey, boarded the bus, and off we went. The bus had a roof which opened to enable us to stand up to view the game, and we stopped at the picturesque Thomson Falls for coffee, then visited a native fruit and vegetable market. Geoffrey warned us not to photograph individual natives, as they look upon cameras as an evil eye, but the whole made a most exotic and colourful picture, then on we went to Outspan for lunch, a beautiful house in a lovely setting, which appeared to be the assembly point for all safaris. After lunch, driving through interesting country, we arrived at our first port of call – the famous Treetops of which everyone has heard.

The original Treetops where Princess Elizabeth was when she was recalled to U.K on the death of her father, was burnt down, and the present hotel in the trees, was built on the opposite side of the water hole. On vacating the bus we were escorted by an armed white hunter, passing a herd of fierce looking water buffalo, to the foot of the ladder which took us to the living quarters. These were rather primitive cabins containing two camp beds and a wash basin. We went up more steps onto the roof where we could look down on the water hole, and had tea which consisted of freshly baked scones and fresh pineapple. There were warthog, funny ugly little animals, which can be quite dangerous, water buffalo and water buck drinking, and cheeky monkeys dashing about on the parapet looking for the chance to snatch a bite off our plates, or, indeed off anyone.

Although Treetops is very touristy, I loved the atmosphere, and the vision I had from reading Karen Blixen, Elspeth Huxley and Sir Laurens van der Post, was becoming a reality.

We were confined to the wooden building from then on until time came for us to leave, and to enable us to see as much of the wildlife as possible, we were up most of the night. Our sighting included, mongoose, genet cat, hyena, water buffalo, warthog, water buck, forest hog and our first rhino. There were no elephants that might, but there were sitings logged of many, and of lion and leopard, it is just a matter of luck. We left Treetops early next morning after tea and biscuits, with the cheeky monkeys and baboons scampering down the stairs from the roof, the door having inadvertently been left open, snatching biscuits as they went flashing past. We breakfasted back at Outspan, feeling rather grubby as there had been no time for a shower, and Geoffrey then drove us about one hundred miles north to Samburu, stopping at Nyeri where we visited Lord Baden Powell's grave, there were a number of graves, I noticed, of people who had met their deaths during the Mau Mau period.

We were all hot and tired, but recovered after lunch when

Geoffrey took us on a game hunt in the park, when we spotted lion, elephant and giraffe, the first honours going to Peta for spotting the lion, then returned to the lodge to enjoy a shower, a drink and a meal altogether.

This is a delightful lodge, well sited on the banks of the river, but we had to be escorted by an armed native, from the main lodge to our chalet, as only two weeks previously, a couple had been charged by a buffalo as they crossed his path in the dark, whilst he was on his way to drink at the river.

We slept under mosquito nets, and had a wonderful night's sleep, were awake at 6.30 a.m. and assembled after breakfast for a game drive. We all got on famously, holding competitions as to who would spot the game first, and saw oryx, ostrich, impala by the score, bushbuck, crocodile, gerenuk. Geoffrey and the driver of another bus spotted the spoor of lion, and the two buses drove in and out of the scrubland looking for him, and as we were going up a rise to get back onto the track we saw something move under an acacia tree. We went back into the scrub, and, to our amazement, found a young, fully grown male feeding on a recently killed buffalo. As we drew nearer, within a few yards, two younger males came to feast. It was a gruesome sight indeed, and I was glad that we had not witnessed the actual kill. Usually it is the lioness who does the hunting and the killing, and the lions the first to eat, but, we were told, lions away from a pride make a kill, in this case, probably two would go for the hind legs to bring the prey down, and the other go for its throat. Nature in the raw indeed, and survival of the fittest. On returning to the lodge for lunch, we had to change a tyre, and the jack was of no use whatever in the soft sand, so it was a case of all hands to the raising of the vehicle.

It had been a very dusty trail, and we were glad to quench our thirst altogether on the balcony, and to watch the beautiful birds, and after lunch, a welcome rest, a swim in the pool, a sunbathe, a shower and change, meeting up again for drinks. Then we witnessed a wonderful spectacle of a lioness climbing a tree to reach the carcass of a kid which had been hoisted up onto a branch as a bait for a leopard. It was, apparently, most unusual for a lioness to take it. After many attempts climbing the tree and trying to grab the bait, which swung on a rope, she was successful in containing it in her paws, and swung on it until the rope broke, and she ran off into undergrowth with her prize. We all watched this in the light of an arc lamp, and in breathless silence.

The Cicadas seem to switch on their chorus as soon as daylight fades, and then the bull frogs join in, and the darkness brings many strange noises and rustlings.

We drove about one hundred and ten miles next day, to Meru, leaving Samburu rather reluctantly, as we all agreed nothing could be quite so good, the service, the situation and the beautifully run establishment were superb. It was my turn to sit next to Geoffrey, we moved around each day. He was very interesting and willing to answer any questions. He told me that on the death of Kenyatta, the Kikuyu would still be the leading tribe. Jomo had, of course obtained Independence for Kenya, but education leaves much to be desired and civilisation must cause a great deal of conflict to these people.

Geoffrey wanted to get married, his fiancee worked in an office in Nairobi, but he had to save up to give his future father-in-law a number of heads of cattle and goats.

We had a bumpy rough ride for four hours stopping once for a magnificent view of Kilimanjaro, with its peak white with snow, and again at a colourful village market of cattle, goats, fruit and vegetables, and felt we ought to be behind the wire with the animals, we created such interest.

I unfortunately had my usual tummy bug, but after a rest

on a game drive, we saw giraffe, herds of zebra, and elephant galore. Here we were housed in Rondaavels, which we found a little restrictve after the spacious room at Samburu. There was a riot of bouganinvilia everywhere, in glorious pink, white, red and purple, and lovely Canna lilies. I was rather unhappy still and retired early, missing supper, and slept well despite getting up twice to investigate ominous roars and grunts, but seeing nothing.

Geoffrey rounded us up after an early breakfast for our last game drive, during which we disturbed a poor Ostrich sitting on a clutch of eighteen eggs, most of which would be stolen by other animals, and she would be lucky to raise three. He took us to see the white rhino which are very nearly extinct. There were two here, purchased by the government from South Africa, and they are in charge of an armed Ranger, who daily releases them from an overnight camp and takes them out to feed. We relaxed in the afternoon, I was feeling much better, thanks, I think, to some of Peta's medicine "Limoten", and Henry painted the view from our Rondaavel, which I have hanging in my bedroom now. He found it a bit tricky painting in watercolours in the humidity, it all dries so quickly. The swimming pool here is not very inviting, looking a dirty green and was rather crowded, so had a shower instead, and sat in my negligee reading my book and glancing at the wonderful panorama, counting eighteen elephant and two buffalo – the latter very close.

This lodge is very busy and has to have two sittings for evening meal, so we did not eat until late.

We took our leave of Meru next day, it had all been most enjoyable, and quite different from Samburu, and headed for Nairobi a long rough and dusty journey of two hundred and thirty miles, stopping at The Isaac Walton at Embu for lunch – a poor place and a worse meal. We ran onto tarmac road after lunch and enjoyed a smooth ride for the rest of the journey, arriving Nairobi about 4 p.m. We all felt sad taking our leave of Geoffrey, who had been so good, kind and helpful, he was planning to go to University to study German.

Back again at the Panafric, we found our rooms and arranged to meet for a drink at 7.30 p.m. and to have our last meal together. It is sad to split up and go our various ways, even though we have been together only six days, we had become a friendly unit, sharing a unique experience, and we all enjoyed each others' company, even Raymon relaxed.Tomorrow Ann and Bill are off to the Seychelles for a week, also Raymon to do some birdwatching, Peta and Sarah go to Malindi, and we to Mombasa.

To our surprise Geoffrey arrived at the hotel next morning, having been detailed to take four of us and a Canadian honeymoon couple to the airport. Although the Kunoni agent was there with our flight tickets, the airport was a shambles, but eventually we took off about 1030 for a 55 minute flight. We piled into the airport bus and called at four hotels dropping people off at each stop, the Nyali, the Mombasa Beach, The Whitesands, where Ann and Bill were staying (they were rather dull company without the girls, but then, I expect we are too), and lastly the Serena Beach which was our destination.

This was designed as a Swahili town, built, of course for the tourist, and owned, we heard, by Jomo Kenyatta. White sands, warm blue seas and waving palms really do exist. There was a young set here, lovely girls, mostly German, who walked along the beach topless, and somehow, didn't look a bit out of place, but the older women were a ghastly sight without their tops.

We found it was a bit expensive here, and did not think we would be able to afford to do many excursions, and we find we have to watch our change, as the boys are wily and ready to make a profit.

We enjoyed an evening meal in the open courtyard which

119

had a central fountain, and a vine-like vegetation heavy with blossom climbing everywhere. It was very hot, and we were quite glad to return to our air conditioned room, but we both agreed, we would enjoy lazing about doing nothing here, the safari had been a bit strenuous.

We rose in a very leisurely manner, which was a pleasant change, and enjoyed breakfast in a spacious cool dining room surrounded by exotic flowers. A boy took two mattresses out onto the beach lounger under the palms, and there we lay all morning. Henry only has to lift a finger, and the beach boy was there to take our order for drinks – what a life!

The Canadian honeymooners were on the beach and asked us to look after their belongings whilst they went for a swim, and they did the same for us. It was a drawback having to take all one's wealth with you, later on at the lodges and hotels, we found that lockers had been installed, which made life much easier. The tide was well out, but we found a deep pool and it was not till later that I found I had burnt, and from then on I wore a cotton hat in the sea, a lot of people wore tee shirts too, as the sun is very strong. There were entertainments most nights, and that evening we watched a display of native dancing, which comes so naturally to the African.

We thought we would catch a bus into Mombasa, but no one could tell us what time it went, so we walked down the road to the stop only to see it driving away. It is quite impossible to run in this climate, so we had to wait three quarters of an hour for the next, and were very glad to sit in the bus in the company of some very cheerful natives. The first word we had learned was "Jambo" the greeting which is given by everyone, and the natives were delighted when we said this. One young man proffered a note for his fare, which gaily blew away in the breeze, much to everyone's delight. the bus stopped and about four of the occupants alighted and gave chase, all laughing merrily with such a lot of chatter. They seem very happy people.

We found a bank, cashed some dollars, sat and had a lovely cold beer and wandered around the town visiting Fort Jesus.

The Portuguese explorer Vasco da Gama arrived on the coast in 1498, and Mombasa was attacked several times during the 16th century. Fort Jesus was built as a stronghold by the Portuguese, but after many battles over the years, they were driven out and finally lost control of the coast and their trading in 1729. It is a vast structure withstanding the ravages of time. We visited the docks, which I felt was rather a mistake, the dockers were such an evil looking ragged lot, then found the Mombasa Club, which we entered and enquired about lunch, despite the notice saying not open to non members. The secretary, a white Kenyan, looking immaculate in white shorts, and smoking a cigarette from a long holder, looked us up and down and decided we were fairly harmless, but we must have looked rather dusty, and we were permitted to collect some chips with which we paid for drinks and sandwiches, and we sat on the balcony looking across the estuary to the sea beyond – it was bliss! There was a group of wealthy looking Asians having drinks, and the place had an air of opulence. Wandering round after lunch, we lost our way, and arrived back at the docks, and seemed to be surrounded by a murderous looking lot, indeed I felt quite nervous, and was glad when we found our way back to the bus. We had a welcome rest on our beds on our return, for Mombasa had been very tiring in the intense heat, then a swim in the lovely warm sea and some delicious pineapple which Kuoni had sent to our room with their compliments. The fruit here is quite delicious.

We spent quite the laziest day ever under a beach umbrella on mattresses, sunbathing, and sea bathing. I really don't know how some people just do this and nothing else on a holiday. We met our Canadian friends for drinks, and after dinner, which was a self service buffet of Kenyan dishes, we watched the native dancing. It is so wonderful to be able to sit out at night under the stars. The wine waiter, all smiles, was delighted to produce a bottle of red wine with a great flourish saying, "This is a surprise, will tell you who from when you have ended it."

It was the Achesons, the Canadians, who had sent it with their compliments.

The Kenyans are all delighted to practice their English, which is now a compulsory language in the schools, and love it when you engage them in conversation and ask them about themselves. One of the boys invited us to his shamba to meet his mother, which we hope to do.

It is intensely hot, and we booked a car planning to move on to Malindi. However hot it is, we are not very good at lying about doing nothing on the beach. Next day being Abel's day off, we took him in the car, armed with a large bag of sweets for his brothers and sisters, who number nine, to his shamba near Kilifi creek. The natives all live in mud huts, and how his family all crowded in I really don't know. Mama did not speak any English, and neither did the little ones, but there was an elder sister who was all smiles, anxious to talk to us, and we had to accept some mealie cakes from Mama. Abel was thrilled to show us off to the rest of the village.

We were not sorry to leave Serena Beach and have our independence once more, and we went down to the actual creek to await the ferry. Whilst waiting we purchased some peanuts and fruit from one of the numerous stalls. Everywhere was pretty filthy and dusty, but as usual the natives were cheerful and happy.

Across the ferry, we drove some thirty-five miles then turned off the main road for Watamu, where we found a super little place called Turtle Bay and had a beer and fresh crab sandwiches. We retraced our drive back to the main road, visiting the ruins of Gedi en route. This had been a prosperous town in the 15th century and it was eerie to walk amongst the walls of the palace, mosques, houses and pillared tombs and the market place. It had been destroyed and left deserted in early 1500.

We drove into Malindi, which looks an interesting town, and found our hotel and a note from Peta and Sarah, warning us of a water shortage, but despite this they had enjoyed their week there. We met some of our fellow visitors, one couple, Jack and Phil, do a lot of underwater photography, despite the fact that he only has one leg. We also met two middle aged sisters named Sue and Snob from Harrogate. We heard good reports of Robinson Island, and planned to visit it in the morning. I spent a poor night, the air conditioning making such a noise, but one cannot survive without it. Justice, our boy, brought us tea at 7 a.m. which we enjoyed on the balcony, but we were appalled at the water shortage, being supplied with a bucketful to swish down the toilet and cannot do any washing. However, we had a swim in the pool before breakfast, packed our swimsuits, sunhats and towels and set off in the right direction for Robinson Island. It was a terrible dirt road, full of potholes for most of the twenty-five miles. Arriving at the ferry, we parked the car and a cheery boatman poled us through mangrove trees with their tangled roots reaching like great claws into the water, and exotic birds flying in and out the trees. On landing, we found a walk covered with plaited palm leaves. I took off my sandals and walked barefoot, but had to put them on again on leaving the covered walk, as the sand was far too hot to walk on. This walk led us to the restaurant and bar, and we immediately ordered a cold beer out of the fridge. The tables and stools were all roughly hewn from mango trees, and we sat under a straw roof, our feet on the sand, looking out to the blue sea, and began our lunch, and what a lunch! The dishes were all local, and the fish freshly caught. We began with a nibble of fried coconut slices, then a dish of oysters, followed by crab and salad, and a short stick to smash the shell, curried fish with rice and pineapple, and coffee served from a tall arab styled pot. All this took nearly three hours and there were raffia covered beds on which to lie in between courses. The owner, a white Kenyan named David Hurd, looking very like Somerset Maugham, wearing nothing but a Kyoti and a beard. He was quite a character and clearly disappointed when we refused his invitation to taste a fish the boys had just caught and cooked in coconut oil, but we just could not cope with more. He shook us by the hand and bade us farewell and we made our way back to the boat and returned to the mainland.

The car was like an oven and a native begged a lift to his shamba on the way to Malindi. Much to our dismay he whistled up two pals, and there we were with three natives in the back. They seemed harmless enough however, and indeed were very helpful when we had difficulty in manoevering the pot holes and on one occasion they got out and filled a hole with branches. The road really was that bad.

On our return to the hotel we found no respite from the water shortage. There had been talk of digging wells, but this is the wrong country to get anything done speedily, if at all. We did manage to have a swim in the pool which was the only way of freshening up, but even the level of that was receeding as the boys took bucketfuls out.

We spent a lazy day after our expedition to Robinson Island. After returning the car to Avis we strolled around the dusty town, bought, after some bargaining, a carving and a Kyoti, and spent the rest of the day under a Kabana (an umbrella made of plaited palm leaves) by the pool, and a beach boy brought us beer and sandwiches. After lunch, when all sensible people were having a siesta, we had a good walk along the beach beside the very muddy looking water.

The reason for the lack of water and the distateful colour

of the sea apparently, was that a lot of trees had been felled along the banks of the river up-stream, resulting in erosion of the banks. We managed to have a word with the Kuoni agent, saying we were dissatisfied with the "super accommodation" we had booked, and suggested they find us alternative accommodation. She did not seem a bit surprised and mentioned "Seafarers" in Turtle Bay. Word came through later that Seafarers had a room so we packed our belongings into the car which we had re-hired and made for Turtle Bay. Here we had a semi detached hut with the minimum of furniture, a shower, a washbasin, mosquito nets and no air conditioning.

We liked the atmosphere very much, and it was run and owned by white Kenyans. Malindi Marine National Park is a protected area of white coral and beaches and clear deep blue lagoons, and this is where we learnt to snorkel. What great pleasure it gave us to explore underwater. Henry was 70 years of age then and he loved it, we would go out to the reef in a glass bottomed boat, dive overboard and wallow in the lovely warm water, and see the most beautiful fish, who appeared near enough to touch, although one never actually managed to do this of course.

Way back in the 15th century the Sheikh of Malindi extended hospitality to Vasco da Gama, when Mombasa became hostile, and Malindi became an important trading centre, and there is a monument – the Cross of Vaso da Gama, presented to the Sheikh by the Portuguese in gratitude for the warm reception extended to the explorer. There are very few relics existing on the coast.

There is an immense Baobab tree near Diani, reputed to be five hundred years old, and is protected from felling. Elephants and trees are Kenya's protected heritage more than man made monuments.

There is another delightful hotel one hundred yards along the beach from Seafarers, to which we often went at lunchtime for the delicious prawn sandwiches. This was run by white Kenyans, the mother and daughter doing most of the work, the husband seeming to spend most of the time at the bar chatting to the elite. They only permitted English to be their guests, Germans were not allowed anywhere near, and the English appeared to be very much of the upper class.

Sitting out on the stoep watching the moon rise is a wonderful sight, and to walk along the warm sand in barefeet chasing the ghost crabs, who only come out at night, scurrying into their holes, is a great entertainment.

All this paradise had to come to an end, so we rose early on our last day – March 8th, to enjoy a last swim in lovely calm water in the lagoon. We returned the car to Avis, and after lunch eight of us, in two buses escorted by Catherine Paul of Kuoni, left for Malindi airport. It is laughable to call it an airport, just a couple of sheds, a runway and a flagpole flying the Kenyan flag. If you happen to be there at sunset you have to stand at attention when the flag is lowered, which we had to do on a later visit.

We stayed a night at the Panafric, which we are getting to know quite well now, and Henry and I strolled into Nairobi to sit at The Thorn Tree for a drink, and watch the world go by. This is truly what one does at The Thorn Tree, everyone assembles there, and there are messages for people who have missed each other, or making arrangements to meet en route for north, south, east, or west.

Nairobi airport was a nightmare, so many queues to join, but the agent and his assistant were wonderful at sorting our luggage through all the hazards, and generally shepherding us into the right queues until we were on board the bus for the Jumbo Jet. We slept intermittently and had a welcome breakfast at 0500 having taken off from Nairobi at 1.20 a.m. local time.

And so another enjoyable experience came to an end,

another adventure finished, and Kenya seemed very far away when we landed at Heathrow with a cold wind blowing and scurries of snow, but what a joy to see Ellinor waiting for us!

—————————————— ∞ ——————————————

CAPE TOWN and the DRAKENSBURGS 1978

We had a pressing invitation from Frank and Jessie to visit them again, and this, our second visit to Cape Town, was just as enjoyable as our first in 1970, they had spent some time with us in U.K in 1971.

We thought it would be nice to explore new ground before arriving in Cape Town, and chose to go to the Drakensburg mountains. With this in view we flew to Johannesburg on February 7th, leaving Benjy with Ellinor for the first time, which puzzled him, as he was usually left at the kennels, and Ellinor drove us to Heathrow. The plane was full and took off fifty minutes late, arriving at Nairobi 8.15 local time, but we stayed on board and went on to Johannesburg. It took us an hour to get through customs, airports are such soulless places in which to have to spend any time. We had arranged with Avis to have a car ready for us to collect, and having done this and signed all the necessary forms, we piled in our luggage and made for the motorway to Machadadorf, stopping at Witbank to get a petrol permit from the Magistrates. Whilst there we found that Henry's overnight bag had been stolen from the back seat. It contained: jerseys, camera, slippers, shaving and toilet bag, credit card and stirling. We thought we had locked the car, but could not have done so. The Africaans police were unhelpful and rude, and we gathered they thought us extremely stupid to leave anything on view, which, of course, we were. This all delayed us for an hour or more, whilst police took fingerprints, then we went shopping to replace the necessities, and eventually set off for the Bambi hotel at Machandadorf.

It was a dull drive over high veldt with miles and miles of maize and we arrived with only just time to have a quick shower before the last orders were taken in the dining room. After enjoying a gorgeous meal we retired to our room absolutely replete. We had to do some telephoning then, to Avis re:cancellation of our credit card, and to send a telegram to Jonathan asking him to deal with the cancellations for us, and a call to Jess to tell of our safe arrival.

It was a joy to hear the bird chorus next morning, and with the welcome warmth of the sun we set off for Pilgrims Rest, scene of a goldrush in the 1870's: one mine was still working as late as 1971.

Descending from the high veldt, we kept to the good road to Kruger Park entering at the Skukuza gate and crossing over the Sabie river. On the way to the camp, we spotted baboon, impala, warthog, giraffe, wildebeest, kudu, zebra and waterbuck, but we had to break the speed limit of 50 mph to enable us to enter the camp. We found our Rondaval, and enjoyed a shower and a drink. I am not very partial to self service except at breakfast time; in the evening I do enjoy waiter service, which we did not have here.

Early morning being the best time to see the animals, we put the alarm on for 5.30 a.m. which we did not really need, as the baboons made such a racket ransacking the dustbins. The only new animals we saw were a pack of ten hyenas, sinister looking scavengers.

We drove through the park making for the Crocodile Gate exit after breakfast. This visit was a little disappointing as there had been heavy rain, and a number of the tracks had been closed, but on our way out we found a narrow dirt road open, which we followed, and round a bend met a hugh bull elephant plodding towards us with no intention, apparently, of leaving the track, on which there was only room for him or for us.

I was terrified, but all Henry said was, "Now don't panic, take a photograph with the window down, you will never get a opportunity like this again."

I thought he was about right there!

I took a photograph and implored dear Henry to "do something quickly!" Henry drove across his front, revved the engine and blew the horn, and it was a great relief to see the bull crash into the undergrowth. I was admonished later when we were looking at the results, saying that I hadn't waited until we were really near enough to see the whites of his eyes – I didn't think elephants had any!

After leaving the park, we drove sixty-two kms to the Swaziland border, and from then on had a nightmare drive in pouring rain on dirt roads, over the mountains at Pigs Peak to Mbabane, and were glad to arrive at the Swazi Spa, a high class hotel where we had a luxurious room, and wallowed in a hot bath. I wore a long skirt for the first time that holiday, and enjoyed the company and the surroundings immensley – all very nice. After a walk around the lovely gardens ablaze with Jacaranda and bouganinvilia, we set off for Hluhlwe National park, a distance of two hundred and fifty kms, a very hot drive indeed, and as usual, made for the pool at the lodge for a cool off, followed by an early night, and awoke refreshed ready for another day. On the way to the Mtubatuba gate we saw white and black rhino, but game was difficult to spot as the grass had grown tall after the heavy rains, and we were in a low vehicle.

We had a good run to Durban, but the weather was cloudy and dull, and we had a little difficulty in finding The Holiday Inn, a strange hotel built with a Mexican influence, where we were booked in. By the time we had a cup of tea in our room it was pouring with rain. Undeterred by this, we donned our waterproofs, and set off for a good walk along the sea front for a breath of the ozone. We hope to drive up into the Drakensburgs tomorrow, but will have to find a tourist office to purchase a map, as all our maps had been in Henry's stolen bag.

There was a most helpful girl in the Tourist office, and she replaced all the maps, guides etc. and we set off for the mountain range in good weather, pausing to admire the view in the Valley of a Thousand Hills, a vast expanse, with not a soul in sight. One wonders how much of this great continent remains still unexplored. We planned to to stop at Nottingham Road for a drink and a sandwich, where Frank had taken us on our previous visit, and were most disheartened to be turned away – too late for service. I called in at a bottle stall and spoke to a very nice young man and asking him where we could eat, he directed us to his own hotel saying we would be very welcome – and indeed we were. The manageress was a Manx girl, and on chatting to two local people we learnt that their daughter was at the Constance Spry school at Windsor, and they were going to see her in July.

Thet set us on the right road and we travelled on the Freeway until just south of Estcourt, and from then on the road deteriorated, and the signposts became non-existent. We climbed into magnificent country with the mountains towering above us, and eventually arrived at the place we had chosen – Champagne Castle Hotel – and to our good fortune they had a room to spare. It was really heavenly there, and reminded us a bit of the Sani Pass Hotel which we visited in 1970. We hoped for a fine day on the morrow, otherwise we would really be lost in the clouds.

The Drakensberg range extends some 960 kms from the Cape Province to Eastern Transvaal, and is known as the spine of Africa. The average height is, I believe, 3000m. There are some tooth-like peaks which the Zulu named *Quathlamba* meaning the barrier of uplifted spears, a very accurate physical description. And there are also the

"Cathedral peaks" and the "Giant's Castle". It didn't need much imagination to see what the names depicted.

The hotel was on the edge of the Giant's Castle Reserve, and we followed a trail to the Duiker Dam and found a stone "hide" where we spent some time watching the variety of birds, but were not lucky enough to see the rare African Lammergeyer. The trail led us below a mountain shaped like the Sphinx, and back to the hotel. We would have been happy to have spent two to three days here, but one does need good weather. We left early next morning in cloud and rain, but ran into better weather as we dropped to Bergville to do some shopping, where I stupidly tripped over some uneven paving and wrenched my knee, and on to the Royal National Park in time for lunch, which we had in the open under the jacaranda tree eating paw-paw sprinkled with lime juice. We were surrounded by bouganinvilia, beds of cannas and agapanthus, hibiscus bushes and lemon trees. It is heavenly there. Despite my groggy knee, we managed a walk in those lovely surroundings, all so spacious and colourful, with tinkling waterfalls everywhere, and lots of *Dassies* (rock rabbit) popping in and out and round the rocks. I was very annoyed to find my camera had jammed, and regret I shall be without any means of photographing until I can get it repaired in Cape Town.

Regretfully we left the mountains, travelling to Harrismith in low cloud and drizzle, driving with head lights on, and got well and truly stuck in the mud. It took us well over two hours to reach Harrismith, a matter of sixty kms, skidding in mud at times one foot deep. So there we were in the mud at the side of the road, with not a soul in sight and no habitation. We both got out and shoved and pushed, but sandals are not the most suitable footwear in these conditions. We were fortunate that a native in a truck came along eventually and assisted us out of the mess, and on arriving at Harrismith we found a garage, moved our cases from the boot to the back seat, and got the boys to mop up the boot, and then went on to Ladybrand. We could not get into The Riverside which had been recommended, so crossed the border into Losotho at Meseru, and made for the Holiday Inn. We were unfortunate, Meseru was packed with delegates attending an Agricultural Conference or with people who had entered for a weekend gambling, there being a large casino in the town. We crossed the border again, which meant four lots of customs, and having to pay to enter, and pay to leave, and eventually found a very crummy joint in Wepaner, with psuedo leopard skins on the floor, and a large Africaans blond ordering the natives servants around. We were relieved to have a roof over our heads, and a hot bath, after the drastic events of the day.

We spent the next day travelling to the coast to East London, through lovely country and into warmer climes, although there was quite a wind blowing, and drove through miles of sugar cane and maize to Port Elizabeth and the Holiday Inn at Wilderness.

The latter part of our journey was a gentle drive in terrific heat, and we enjoyed a walk along the beach, and indeed, in the surf to wash the mud off our sandals. No wonder this is called the Garden Route, everywhere is so luxuriant. We bought a pineapple being offered by some cheery native children by the roadside. Henry had a penknife so we were able to enjoy it there and then, and had a sandwich at Stormy River Bridge. The sea and the beach looked beautiful at Plattenburg, but it clouded over and was very windy when we reached the Wilderness for the night. The weather was no better next day, but we spent a relaxed morning in Knysna, walking round the Heads, and found a delightful hotel on the shore of one of the lakes for our lunch, then made our way back to Wilderness. We had a long run ahead of us so planned to make an early start.

It is March 22nd, and Linda's baby is due today, she and

Jonathan were very much in our thoughts. We called at George, Mossel Bay and Swellendam, where we found a quiet spot on the roadside. Well, it was quiet when we pulled up, but suddenly we were surrounded by five new cars being driven by natives, who were, they told us delivering them to Stellenbosch. We decided to stay the night at Hermanus at a hotel named Riviera – not a good choice, its name belied it, so changed to the Birkenhead next day having first telephoned Frank and Jess, and heard the wonderful news of Sam's arrival. It is incredible to realise we now have five grandsons! This hotel was super, the weather again smiled on us and we spent the afternoon in and out of the sea, and met a couple from Hanley Castle.

On Frank's recommendation we called at an old farmhouse at Houhoeck for lunch on the way to Cape Town, and arrived at Mulvihal Road in the afternoon, to find Frank washing his car on the lawn, so that no precious water would be wasted. We had a great welcome, and it is so nice to be here again. Trish arrived with her family – two boys now, then Robert and Helen who were married soon after our last visit, and now have a boy Michael, and a baby girl, Wendy. Together with the family, and two friends from Taunton, we were quite a large party that evening. Sadly there was no Granny Teagle, she had died two years ago, and we missed her cheerful presence.

It is fun to enter into the social round once more. A visit to the Kensington races was interesting and enjoyable, but not one of us had any luck. The natives still have their own enclosure, but I am sure this will change. Church with Frank and Jess at 7 a.m. Walks on the beach and swims in the sea. Frank took me to the Kodak building where I left my camera to be repaired, and Henry, who has had a nasty cough, paid a visit to the doctors who diagnosed Sinusitis and prescribed antibiotics and an inhalant.

We were all present at Robert and Helen's on their sixth wedding anniversary, when they received the news that they were being transferred to London in June; they were so excited. We were delighted for them, and look forward to seeing more of them.

David Sonnenburg, a friend of Peter and Ellinor's, and who was a guest at their wedding, arranged to collect us and he and his wife, Sue, entertained us to drinks at their flat.

We watched W. Province play Natal at Newlands cricket ground, and lunched with Mike and Val Odling at Stellenbosch, whom we knew from Pontypool, we also met up with Maureen and Royce Bowen, the Mostyns, the Howes and the Yates. And so continued the social round, renewing old friendships and meeting new friends, and visiting the Baxter theatre to hear a Pianoforte Recital of Beethovens works.

One morning Jessie took us into the city hoping to show us the new Nico Melan theatre but found it firmly closed, as anti-apartheid demonstrators were demanding performances before mixed audiences.

Robert and Helen had a fisherman's cottage lent to them for a holiday and we joined them at Arniston, a pretty fishing community. The cottage was a bit primitive – although it boasted plumbing of sorts there was no electricity and we had to use candles and cook by Calor Gas. We played darts, I recall, by the light of a standard gas lamp. The evening meal was usually a brie out in the open. The swimming was good, and the countryside provided lovely walks. Henry painted a watercolour of the area, which he gave to Jessie.

We flew to Johannesburg on March 15th, and on to Heathrow, to be met with cold winds, and snow. It will take us a while to get acclimatised and settle down again to the domestic routine. And so, we came to the end of our visit, I wonder when we shall all meet up again. As usual, it has all been so enjoyable.

MAURITIUS and SEYCHELLES 1979

Islands seem to have a great attraction for us, we had heard so much about Mauritius we decided to explore it first then go on to the Seychelles.

We left Glebe House in January and as Peter and Ellinor were due to go on a skiing holiday we put Benjy in the kennels at Maidenhead, much to his disgust. But at least he had Barty for company and it was only for a week as Ellinor would be collecting both dogs on her return. We explained all this to Benjy, but it did nothing to cheer him up and he still looked miserable, which makes me feel so guilty.

There had been some snow with more forecast so we expected bad driving conditions, but it proved to be not too bad. Peter had told us of a garage where we could leave the car for a week. He was going to collect it later and having deposited it the proprietor took us to the airport. Everything went smoothly, but oh! it was such a long journey, sixteen hours flight with an alteration of four hours on our watches. With one stop at Nairobi and one at Seychelles, there seemed endless officialdom to go through, then a long drive by taxi, eventually arriving at The Morne Brabant Hotel, situated on a peninsula on the west coast which was about the farthest point from the airport. It was all worthwhile, the sea was lovely and warm and clear, promising good snorkelling.

This is a gorgeous lush island, volcanic, of some seven hundred and twenty square miles. The Portuguese were the first to discover it in 1510, then the Dutch came in 1598, and named it Mauritius after their Prince Maurice of Nassau, when the only occupant was the now extinct Dodo. They started growing sugar which is the main source of revenue to this day. The Dutch left in 1710 then the French occupied the island and were responsible for the lay out of the capital Port Louis. The English conquered the island in 1810 and allowed the French to stay, thus everyone speaks French or the local Creole. Enough of the history lesson.

There was no car available on our first attempt to hire, but we were able to book one for the next two days, so in the meantime we spent our day lazing, bathing and snorkelling, then spent an hour in a glass bottomed boat viewing the fishes and the coral. The latter, we thought, was nothing like as colourful as the reef off Watamu on the Kenyan coast.

Fresh pineapples were purchased from a native on the beach, who expertly peeled and hacked them with a long handled knife, leaving the top leaves as a handle; all this done in a minute. We have had bad nights so far, being hot and sticky with a few mosquitos buzzing around; these always attack Henry unfortunately.

After a lovely breakfast of paw paw, pineapple, bacon, egg and coffee, we found that a Mini had been reserved for us and off we went, taking the coast road to Port Louis, some forty miles. We had difficulty in finding parking, which seems to be a problem the world over, the place was milling with people, donkeys, carts and cars, and the roads were awful. We visited the covered market, there is always something very attractive about markets, and although this one was extremely smelly and dirty it was nevertheless, fascinating. One side was selling an amazing assortment of spices (of which I bought some nutmeg and saffron) and a large variety of fruit and vegetables, and the other side displayed gorgeous coloured materials, T shirts, scarves and handicrafts. We emerged from the market and stood on a corner, wondering where we could get something to eat when a very nice young man accosted us, asking if he could be of any assistance. He guided us to indian rest house, and showed us the direction to the Museum. We were so grateful, the restaurant was cool and we immediately ordered two beers each, and the waiter brought what he called "a snack", two spicy pieces of chicken on sticks on a bed of salad, all rather hot. We found the museum and duly inspected the very clumsy looking Dodo and other artefacts, and then found the Pamplemousse Botanical Gardens, which were a delight. There was a great variety of Palm trees, one of which, whose name I have forgotten, blooms every sixty years then dies. The ponds were covered with giant waterlilies, the leaves of which were like large round trays, and we saw tortoises which were one hundred years old. A native gardener befriended us and took us to see Nutmegs, Cloves, Betel and Cachou nuts, the twenty four hour lily and lotus flowers growing. A most enjoyable day, and we enjoyed a seafood buffet out in the open at the hotel. We slept well that night, but were concious of a stormy wind which continued throughout the day, and it didn't take much imagination to think what a cyclone would be like. We bade farewell to a couple from Maidenhead who were on their way to Australia, and made for the mountains, climbing up to the central plateau. We called at Curpipe a pleasant residential town with some magnificent houses and good shops; drove through tea plantations and saw Le Grande Bassin – a water filled crater to which the Hindus trek on one of their religious festivals. It poured with rain whilst we there, in fact, we had to pull up as it was quite impossible to drive and we caught only an occasional glimpse of the mosque. Everywhere we went the people were so pleasant and helpful, which helps to make everything so much more enjoyable, but it was nice to get back to the hotel for a swim and a freshen up for the evening. After dinner we visited The Meridian a neighbouring hotel where there was a casino, but after a little play we decided this was not for us.

After a wet night we awoke to find that two waterfalls had appeared down the mountain opposite our cabin. We returned the car and strolled around and, in general, spent a lazy day feeding the birds on our balcony and trying to photograph them. There were some very pretty ones with red eyes and black crests, and lovely small yellow ones, and plenty of sparrows which look very much the same as ours. The soos are lovely tall trees that make a swishing, whispering noise with their feathery leaves, in the breeze. We spent a pleasant evening in the company of a dutch couple who ran a cattle farm in Zambia, and were here enjoying two weeks holiday.

The air conditioning in our cabin is excellent and when I emerge to the outside, my spectacles steam up. There is, apparently, a cyclone centred over Plaisance which is making the weather here rather unpleasant, with showers and gusty winds.

We packed up and left on Monday Feb 5th and were driven to the airport in a minibus in the company of four people from Blackpool who were on their way home, and a Meteorologist from London who was having a session studying the weather in the Seychelles. On arrival we were driven to our hotel the Northolme, but were disappointed in our room, a large wooden one with no air conditioning. After a dreadful first night, which was very hot, and during which were kept awake by a whining dog, we complained, and the owners said they would be able to move us into a bungalow in the grounds on the morrow.

The hotel itself is a very interesting place. Originally it was the home of a tea planter, and has distinguished names on some of the doors: Ian Fleming, Compton Mackenzie and Noel Coward. It has its own private beach, from which the swimming and snorkelling is magnificent, but, unfortunately, they appear to be suffering from a plague of cockroaches, and the Rentokil gang were busy spraying the rockery.

We were duly installed in the bungalow which had a communal balcony with the adjoining section, and it was very pleasant to sit outside and view the wonderful sunsets.

Our hire car was a Honda this time, and we drove along the coast to Victoria, the capital, the outstanding feature being a victorian clock tower in the square, and walked around the town to get our bearings. It was not until the next day we got a little more adventurous, driving first to Victoria, up over the mountains through the Sans Souci pass and into the most beautiful and lush country. We took it all very leisurely, stopping to appreciate the views and call in at a tea factory. Unfortunately there was not much doing there, it was probably their lunch break so we dropped down to Mahi Beach, where the hotel is a monstrosity. We took a boat over to the Isletts where we had a freshly caught "Job" fish, which was delicious, and so back to the hotel at a leisurely 20 mph, which is the most we ever do, indulged in a lovely bathe, drinks at the bar and dinner in the company of one Cathy Cadwallader – whose husband is in oil – and a couple from Hongkong.

We travelled with Speedbird this holiday, for the first time, and were invited to a buffet of fish dishes at the Reef which was quite delicious. En route we called at the Botanical Gardens to see the beautiful orchids. After a lazy day spent swimming, looking, reading, and sunbathing, we went on another exploration. I was suffering from a tummy bug which improved after taking remedial pills. We drove to Victoria, across the spine of the island *Les Conelles* over to the west coast, which is prettier and less developed, but not for long, one fears, down to Police Bay, on to Roche, and over the Sans Souci pass. It does not take long to cover the Island, and we felt we had explored it all.

We had to sort out our luggage as we were only allowed to take 15lbs each on the light plane, and the agent took charge of our large cases and housed them at the Reef to await our arrival for our flight home. We boarded a Cessna which took eight passengers, and flew above a beautiful blue sea to Praslin. A taxi took us to the Paradise Hotel. It was perfect and our only regret was that we had not come here sooner.

Davie, the agent, introduced himself and booked us for one excursion to La Digue and another to the island of Cousin. After a good night's sleep with no noisy air conditioning, but an overhead fan, we were taken to St. Ann jetty, where a dozen of us boarded a boat for the hour sail to La Digue. Here, we were met by ox-carts, each carrying four passengers. There were no motor vehicles on this tiny island. We were taken to see a Coconut factory owned by a German who employed one hundred and twenty natives. Every part of the coconut is used, the nut, the copra pressed to extract oil and the fibre for matting etc. After a welcome drink and a Creole lunch we strolled around and found, to our delight, a boatbuilders yard, where four natives were building a cargo boat from Tamarak wood. We watched and chatted with them for some time. This was a lovely day which we enjoyed so much. I lost my straw hat on the return sail, the breeze whipped it off and it sailed through the air, landed on the sea, and floated merrily away, much to everyone's amusement.

The Vallee de Mai is situated in the National Park in the centre of Praslin. Up to 1930 it was untouched virgin forest and in 1945 the government took it over. The entrance is flanked by the famous Coco-de-Mer trees and notices requesting visitors to take only photographs and to leave only footprints. We followed the trail which was sometimes very precipitous, with lovely views of the beautiful clear blue sea and the neighbouring island, *Silhouette*. The forest was lush and green with many geckos darting up the tree trunks, and lizards of many colours basking in the sun. The south side was steep and not easily accessible, and here was the nesting site of the Seychelles Swiftlet, which we saw flying around the viewing lodge. We also saw black parrott, the blue fruit pigeon and the sunbird: an ornothologists paradise, and a place of utter tranquility.

Next day we were duly collected, taken to Grand Anse, and again boarded a boat which took us a four hour's sail to Cousin, where it was impossible to beach, but local boatmen collected us and took us ashore. The party was divided into French speaking and English speaking, and, incredible as it may seem, our guide named Michael had trained at Dale Fort and had come direct to Cousin from the Island of Skokholm! We spent a fascinating afternoon, seeing and hearing the Brush Warbler, the fairy tern, who lay their eggs on any convenient branch or wall with no nest, tern, bridled tern, white-tailed tropic bird, huge frigates, shearwaters, sooty tern, and numerous green and pink lizards. We had to follow our guide in complete silence and as quietly as possible to avoid disturbing the birds, and arrived back, wet, thirsty, and very tired.

Sadly, our last day arrived. We would have loved to have spent more time here, and we spent the day swimming, snorkelling, sunbathing and strolling around. For the latter I had to wear sandals as I found the berries from the soo trees painful to bare feet.

The plane service was not operating, owing to lack of fuel, and we had to wait to hear how and when we would be able to leave the island, but nothing seems to matter here. We awoke to a terrific thunderstorm at 6 a.m. and were told we would be leaving Praslin by boat for Mahe at 5 p.m. We hoped fervently the weather would improve. At the jetty, we had to wait two hours for our craft, which, to our horror, proved to be a deep sea fishing vessel with a partially covered cabin, with the pilot and his mate perched above us on a platform.

The engine was powerful and we shot away from the jetty with a great roar, we found it impossible to sit comfortably and had to stand, clinging on for dear life, as we were tossed from side to side skimming over the water.

The sun disappeared rapidly and we travelled in complete darknesss with no navigation lights! We were very relieved to see the lights of Victoria and we passed the QE2 in the harbour, looking a picture ablaze with lights. What a journey! There was a taxi waiting to take us to The Reef, not our favourite hotel, it being too big, and too noisy, and I was suffering from temporary deafness brought on by the continual roar of the engines of our craft.

At the airport next day the plane took off an hour late and the flight seemed long and tedious. The Captain announced he would have to alight at Rome to refuel, which was not scheduled, but he had met strong headwinds, and the conditions at Heathrow were poor.

During the flight Henry had the misfortune to tear his trousers on the metal of the ashtray on the arm of the seat and he went to see the Air Hostesses who thought it all very amusing, asked if his wife was accompanying him, and provided him with safety pins. Armed with these, under the cover of a blanket, I managed to codge the three-cornered tear together. We since discovered, that a relative of Liz's was sitting adjacent to us and had witnessed the incident!

Conditions changed and we landed at Heathrow at 0930, went through the formalities with ease, telephoned Ellinor, who came to collect us, accompanied by Nick and Tim. They had had a good time skiing in Austria, the dogs had behaved but the bad news was that Alastiar was in hospital with Perthes disease.

We have had a wonderful time, have no wish to visit the Seychelles again, but would relish another visit to The Paradise Hotel on Praslin.

NAIROBI and SECOND SAFARI:1980

We followed the usual routine, driving to Ellinor's, leaving the car and Benjy, who, incidentally now appears to enjoy being left with Barty for company. The meals on board did not help an awful bout of indigestion from which I was suffering. However, we touched down at 0730 and even that early in the morning the wave of hot air greeted us on leaving the aircraft, and I felt like kissing the ground, as the Pope always does on landing in a different country.

We travelled by Speedbird this time, and the agent met us, took us to the Serena Hotel and briefed us on our safari. We were only allowed one small case, so had to do a bit of sorting out, our large case to be left at the hotel and collected later. After this we had a welcome bath and enjoyed a drink on the patio accompanied by the chorus of cicadas, and chatted to a Kenyan at our table, who turned out to be a doctor who had qualified in Bombay and Edinburgh, and who had worked in Amsterdam, Brussels, and the Soviet Union, and now held a government post in Nairobi. One meets such interesting people when travelling.

In the morning we met our driver – Joel, and our companions, a retired couple named Woollard, who were as dull as we were although we learnt later that they were on their honeymoon, which surprised us. We set off on a long, tiring, hot, journey. About thirty miles out of Nairobi one comes to the lip of the great Rift Valley, which is a crack in the earth's crust, and stretches some 4000 miles between Lebanon in the north and Mozambique in the south. The road drops two thousand feet to the floor of the valley, and the valley is rarely more than thirty miles wide.

We drove to Lake Nakuru, one of many soda lakes in the valley and home to millions of flamingoes. Approaching the grey soda flats, one is aware of a growling murmer; the sound of the mass of birds feeding. As they become aware of ones approach they panic to take off – a clumsy proceedure – but once airborn they become creatures of grace and look like a huge pink cloud. The water apparently enters the lake at three inlets and there is no outlet so the build up of minerals gives the water a high alkaline content. There is an algae which thrives on the content and the flamingoes, in turn, thrive on the algae. Amongst this mass there were dainty avocets, cormorants, pelicans and the ugly maribou stork.

We lunched in Nakuru, the fourth largest town in Kenya, and drove on to Lake Victoria. This lake is divided in half by Uganda and Tanzania, with very little of it in Kenya and we stayed at the Sunset Hotel at Kisumu. The hotel was well named and we witnessed the most magnificent sunset. The lake looked beautiful when we awoke, very busy with fishermen in canoe-like boats and cormorants covering the branches of bare trees on the waters's edge. We drove to a more interesting bay – Kendu Bay – which was a hive of activity with fishermen coming and going with much shouting and laughing, and the womenfolk unloading the catches. We watched a pied kingfisher diving for fish. We were, according to the itinerary, due to go to Lake Sindi, but Joel, new to the area, could not find it, so we told him to forget it and we went on to Homa Bay, were we had a drink, bought some bottles, and had a picnic lunch. We soon became an object of great interest to the village children, one seems to collect them whenever there is a stop. After we had eaten we gave them the rest of our sandwiches and drove on to see the Soapstone workers at a Community Centre, only to find the place closed down The carving was still being done by the people of the village though, and we were invited to see the products, and, of course, to buy. On the whole we were not impressed with the work and returned to the bus to find, to our dismay, that it would not start. Joel proved to be no mechanic, so there we were, stuck in the middle of nowhere, surrounded by the inhabitants of the entire village. One toothless old crone grabbed my hand through the open window, young matrons showed off their babies, one admired my hair, and one invited me to share her home. I was suffering from my usual upset tummy, and was getting distinctly worried as to what their toilet facilities were like! We were stuck there for an hour not daring to venture out of the bus. The menfolk looked very aggressive – whilst Henry, Ted (Woollard) and Joel tinkered with the engine. It was a great relief to hear the sweet sound of it, albeit not very smooth, and we headed for Kericho, the heart of the tea country and put up at the Tea Hotel, a delightful haven after such a traumatic day.

We visited the plantation after breakfast, acres of lush green bushes dotted with the heads of the pickers, who were plucking the topmost young leaves and tossing them into the wicker baskets slung on their backs.

On leaving Kericho we looked forward to spending two days at Keekorok, a renowned Safari Lodge, but had only travelled one mile when the bus again broke down, and on our suggestion (Joel was at his wits end, and just didn't know what to do) we drove back to the Tea Hotel, and whilst Joel spoke to the Sikh owner of the local garage, who said he would fit a new carburretor in one hour, Henry telephoned Mr. Lawrence in Nairobi, and told him, in no uncertain terms, what we thought of it all.

So off we went once more, and had a most trying journey, once off the tarmac and onto rough track, the vehicle stopped a few times, but Joel persevered and drove to Bomet where he knew there was a telephone, with the intention of contacting Keekerok, but the one and only telephone was out of order! The bus behaved well after Joel had put a few pints of oil into the sump, but we were all tense and expecting further stops. Thankfully, we entered the Reserve with a further sixty kms to do to the actual lodge. Once through the gates, we saw gazelle, topi, buffalo, zebra, and baboon, giraffe, two lioness, two lion, five cubs, wildebeest, and Hartebeest, and arrived at the Lodge worn out, at 1830. We were shown to a pleasant cabin and after a bath and a gin and tonic, we felt more human and ready for a meal.

Keekerok is one of Kenya's oldest lodges, quite delightful with an artificial waterhole to attract elephant and buffalo, which we watched after dinner. One feels in some reserves, as we did here, that we were the guests of the animals. There is a tented camp within the reserve here – The Govenor's Camp, which would be quite an experience, as one would be right among the noises and the smells of the animals, although here, there were piles of dung on the grass outside our cabin, denoting the presence of a nocturnal visitor. We thought the notice which read "Do not go beyond this point" should be turned round for the benefit of the animals.

We went game viewing before breakfast, the best time to go, and saw, apart from those already mentioned, seventeen elephant – my favourite – and two rhino.

I enjoy the Kenyan breakfasts which are self service, with lovely fresh fruits and good coffee. We spent the rest of the morning lazily watching the beautiful swallows flying in and out of the eaves. They have black and white striped breasts, orange heads and blue wings with an orange patch on the lower back. We went game viewing again after lunch, but this is not a good time to go, as all sensible animals are sheltering in what shade they can find.

Henry held another telephone conversation with Lawrnece in Nairobi, and we found in the morning that Joel had been provided with a fresh bus. We left Keekerok rather sadly, as it was one of the nicest lodges we had encountered. We passed herds of zebra and wildebeest, and picturesque Masai warriors driving their cattle to new pastures. The Masai are the handsomest and proudest of Kenya's nomads, tall and upright, they wear red ochre robes and carry broad pointed spears. Their hair is often tied in small knots and shines with grease, and their greatest pride is their cattle.

We had hoped to see leopard and cheetah, but with no luck. Instead, driving through a thicket of acacia, we came upon a herd of about fifty elephant, who suddenly seemed to be all around us, the elders guarding about six young.

On arrival at Nairobi we said farewell to the Woollards, who had not been the brightest of companions, but, despite everything, we had enjoyed the trip. But then we enjoy most things. I am sure Joel was glad to be back and to shed his responsibilites. he had had a most unhappy time. Roy Lawrence came to see us at the hotel, and we related all the mishaps on safari and told him we expected some compensation.

We had a twenty minute flight in a Focke Friendship to Malindi, and a bus to Seafarers, and found that we had been allotted a hut at the end of a newly erected row nearest the sea. This was our second visit, and we felt very much at home. The government had taken the camp over on a seven year lease since our last visit, and we did have the impression that it was not so well run, the natives not so efficient as the owners, but we were pleased to see that they were still around, living in the grounds.

We knew our way around here, and were able to plan to do a lot more, first going into Malindi to hire a car, which we drove back. We booked a sail on a native Dhow; a walking tour with Mark Easterwood, a Botanist, two nights on the Island of Lamu, and hoped to go Robinson Island again.

In between these activities, we enjoyed the snorkelling, the best time to go being before breakfast, and there were days spent in and out of the sea, sunning ourselves and partaking of the delicious prawn sandwiches for lunch at Ocean Sports, which we found to be just as good as on our last visit. We had interesting company at Seafarers too, a recently widowed lady named Mrs.Hopcroft, whose son was fruit farming near Kilifi, and an entertaining couple named Curtis from Nairobi. This is quite a resort for the white Kenyans.

The day we spent on Robinson Island was just as good, and the bumpy drive to the mangrove swamps had not improved. We parked the car and were poled through the swamps in a boat accompanied by two schoolboys who chatted to us in English, wanting to exchange names and addresses and for us to take their photographs – in fact we had a job to get rid of them. At the bar we met the owner, David Hurd, who had been in Kenya twenty-five years, and on the island since 1964. The meal was superb, starting with fried coconut, fried shrimps, small oysters, a large crab with salad, fish soup, grilled snapper, pineapple, and coffee flavoured with cinnamon and ginger. We were glad to lie on the rest beds in between courses, and we staggered back to the boat, managing to give the boys the slip. On our return to the car we found it was like an oven inside, although we had parked it under the shade of a tree, but it soon cooled down once we got going with the windows down, and we were glad of a cooling swim on our return.

For the trip on the dhow, we had to be at the jetty by 9 a.m. where we joined a party of thirteen others, all English, Bob, our host, and a crew of four natives.

Unfortunately, there was no wind, so we had to motor south of Malindi, weaving in and out of the coral, but always in sight of land. We went ashore onto a small beach for a picnic, and headed for where primitive loos had been erected in the woods. Bob escorted us on a short walk which was quite difficult over rough coral, through thick shrub, to a crater where odd bones had been found. In fact Bob showed us a mound of coral in which bovine bones could clearly be seen. On arriving back at the beach we found a feast had been prepared, the natives having cooked kingfish and Tunny which they had caught en route, and we lunched off these, accompanied by salad and baked potatoes which they cooked over the fire. This was followed by fresh pineapple, bananas and coffee. Whilst we ate we had the company of four herons and two ugly maribous.

We had to use the motor on our return until we reached the reef when the lateen sail was unfurled and the crew brought out a drum and sang a rather monotonous but infectious tune, encouraging us to sing some sea shanties. In the party were two girls, and I remember being most intrigued, as were the male members of the party, at the display of a tatooed butterfly on one girl's thigh, which was exposed when she lent over the boat.

On landing we found, to our dismay, that we had a flat tyre, and suspected it had been deliberately deflated by arab urchins who immediately surrounded us and offered assistance. We managed to inflate it despite the fact that Henry was not feeling too good – the latter end of the trip had been very rough and we were glad to reach Seafarers for a quiet drink. The day had been most enjoyable and quite an experience.

For our trip to the Island of Lamu we were up early to hand over the car, and the small plane carrying eight passengers took off at 9.15 a.m. We were quite unable to converse during the noisy flight and landed on Mande Island about 10 a.m. Then we were taken across to Lamu by boat through mangrove swamps, where we were met by guides, one of whom attached himself to us and introduced himself as "Mohammed the Good". He escorted us to the one and only hotel – Petley's. I do not know how old the hotel is, but it was named after the first owner, one Percy

151

Petley, who is said to have thrown unruly women down the stairs, and killed a leopard with his bare hands!

Lamu is a fascinating Island, though extremely smelly. There are no motor vehicles apart from the District Commissioner's land rover, and everything is transported by mule. On walking through the narrow streets one has to stand in doorways to allow heavily laden mules and donkeys to pass, and one is greeted everywhere by smiling natives, indeed some shake you by the hand and bid you "welcome to Lamu."

It is hard to know what the natives do except fish a little and talk a lot. There are woodcarvers doing the most beautiful and intricate work – which is visible on the doorways of many houses – lovely studded doors dating back to the 18th century, but even the modern ones retain the style and form of ancient traditions. There were boatbuilders, the work all being done by hand even to the making of the nails. It was fascinating to watch them at work, and they were clearly pleased to explain anything we asked. One builder left his work to show us the store of wood he had soaking in the sea, and how he selected particular shaped pieces he needed.

Lamu was the centre of the slave trade, and the building in which these poor captured souls were kept prior to being shipped to England and America is still standing. In the museum there is a description and drawings of slave ships showing how the slaves were chained down and packed in, it is not surprising that few survived the voyage. It also houses two magnificent ceremonial carved ivory horns.

The women are swathed in black buibuis, with only their eyes visible. There is a fine mosque where infidels, modestly dressed and without shoes, are allowed to enter; also an old fort which is now the prison, which one photographs at the peril of becoming an inmate. We found a pleasant beach good for bathing, about three kms walk away, which was covered with shells of all shapes and sizes, and that is Lamu!

We spent a very noisy night. They did not appear to have a particular closing time, judging from the late night inhabitants of the bar, but we wouldn't have missed this visit for anything; in fact it was the highlight of this holiday, but two days was quite sufficient. So we bid Mohammed the Good farewell, boarded the Piper aircraft which took us to Malindi, where a car was waiting to take us to the peace and quiet of Seafarers.

We spent a gorgeously lazy day, and on the following day Davine – the Speedbird agent – showed us a telex from Roy Lawrence offering us a free visit to Treetops on the 20th, which was in six days time, but having already been there, we were not enamoured with the idea. However, we spent the next six days snorkelling, sleeping, swimming, eating and walking; enjoying every minute of the lovely sunshine. On our return to Nairobi we were once again housed at The Jacaranda Hotel. We arranged with Roy to visit The Ark instead of Treetops. We took a bus into the city, visited the bank, sauntered round the shops, then sat and had a drink at The Thorn Tree, which is something every visitor to Nairobi must find time to do, to watch the cosmopolitan world go by.

On returning to our hotel we found an invitation from Brenda and John Thornton – Margaret Galbraith's brother and sister-in-law who live in Nairobi, to dine with them on the following Saturday, which I am sure we will enjoy. I tried to get Saen on the telephone – she is the daughter of our friend Dorothy Roberts who lives in Haverfordwest, and whose husband, Jake is manager of the Bloc Hotels, his office being in the famous Norfolk Hotel – but to no avail. We took a taxi to the museum, it being far too hot to walk, and spent an interesting three hours, then walked *poli-poli* (Swahili for slowly) to the Norfolk.

This is the oldest hotel in Nairobi. It was originally a wooden bungalow, and opened its doors to the public on

Christmas day 1904 when the town consisted of one cart track from the railway station, with several *dukas* (small shops) on either side, an office and a store. The track became Government Road, and was renamed Moi Avenue after Independence in October 1978. The train from Mombasa arrived only twice a week bringing a stream of people for the game hunting, and The Norfolk became known as "The house of Lords" because of the number of titled people who stayed there and made it home from home.

By 1908 The Norfolk had expanded its accommodation to thirty four bedrooms and two cottages. It boasted baths with hot and cold water and electric light. lions were often seen in the swamps in front of the hotel, and frogs emitted a chorus from dusk to dawn. The verandah was used as an office by anyone who did not possess one, and on it, meetings of the Fire Brigade and the Turf Club were held, and attracted many famous people in the literary world such as Robert Ruark, Ernest Hemingway and Elspeth Huxley. The hotel still retains its colonial atmosphere, and here we sat enjoying a beer, avocados fresh from the tree and a ham sandwich. We walked around the inner courtyard with its aviaries, and collection of old vehicles. Now, where the lions used to sleep, is overlooked by very modern University buildings of striking architecture. The students had all been banned during our visit, for their riots of a week or so ago, when they complained about the food, and they were forced to pay damages. There was a message from Saen to say she would contact us on our return from The Ark.

We were collected by a UTC bus and met our companions for The Ark, John and Elizabeth Coventry from Malawi, who were retiring to Malmesbury. We stopped at Thomson Falls and the market, as we had done three years ago, and arrived at Aberdare Country Club for lunch, after which we joined a party of Swiss in a larger bus and made for The Ark along a rough bumpy road.

The lodge was very well appointed, and one could view

the animals visiting the waterhole from a huge picture window or an undergound look-out. There were fifteen elephant at the salt lick when we arrived, and we settled in our cabin, which was more roomy than Treetops, and sat and watched buffalo, warthog, Gennet cat, hog, buck, bushpig and elephant. A lot of guests stay up all night for game watching, but we retired, arranging with the watchman to buzz us three times if there was anything out of the ordinary to see. This went off at 1 a.m. I awoke Henry, snatched a blanket to put round me, and dashed to the viewpoint just in time to see the rear end of a leopard, the first I had ever seen. Henry did not see anything as he stopped to put his trousers on – much to his disgust. The buzzer went off again at 5 a.m. and this time we were both rewarded with the sight of a Bongo which is a rare nocturnal antelope, with a beautiful glossy fawn, black and cream coat, and long horns. His legs looked like a guardsman's polished boots, and we watched him for over half an hour. It was not worth going back to bed so we washed, dressed, and watched the dawn break over Mount Kenya, which was a wonderful sight. After breakfast we returned to the Aberdare Country Club and took the bumpy road back to Nairobi, feeling well rewarded. Roy Lawrence had lived in Kenya fifteen years and had never seen a Bongo.

Saen called for us after we had had a day's rest, and entertained us on the Norfolk verandah, where we enjoyed VIP treatment, being guest of the manager's wife, and Jake joined us for a short while. Incidentally, the following Christmas, there was a bomb explosion at the hotel, planted by an arab, which destroyed quite a bit of the original facade, which was very sad. We were worried when we heard the news on the radio at home and on contacting Dorothy we learnt that Jake and Saen had been fortunate. They stopped off to visit friends whilst on their way to the celebrations at The Norfolk, and consequently missed the explosion.

We spent a very pleasant evening with the Thorntons, but it struck me as sad that they had to employ a guard to be on duty all night, despite the fact that they had two dogs – such is life in Nairobi! We entertained them at our hotel the next night – our last one.

So it was to the airport again next day, which is getting quite familiar, and we now know where we can collect Avocados and coffee to take home.

After an all night flight, we arrived at Heathrow in cold wet weather, Ellinor came to collect us, and we received a terrific welcome from all, including Benjy, and drove home to settle down again until the next time.

SRI LANKA and MALDIVES 1982

We travelled with Kuoni this time leaving home on Jan 16th earlier than usual for us, and after following the usual proceedure of leaving the car and the dog with Ellinor and Peter we boarded the plane at 8.30 p.m. called at Dubai for fuel and altered our watches three hours. We crossed the Arabian desert at 25000 feet, landed at Muscat where we had to stay on board then left for Colombo at 9.50 a.m. altering our watches another one and one half hours, and flew across the Indian ocean arriving at Colombo at 3 p.m. Am getting quite blasé about flying. Colombo airport was absolute turmoil, terribly hot with no air conditioning. Nobody appeared to be in charge of anything and we went behind the scenes and collected our own luggage, and left the airport on a Kuoni bus arriving at our hotel the Meriviere Kalutara at 7 p.m. quite exhausted. Despite noises in the night, caused by a cricket in the fresh air grille and the ghekos scooting over the walls with their clogs on, we had a good night, but were awakened early by the pantry boys. Their room unfortunately was next door to ours, but it was wonderful to see the palms, the blue sea, the beach and the sunshine. We spent the day lounging in the sun recovering from our long flight, and although I was careful I caught the sun. The next day was a public holiday being a full moon on which no alcohol was sold.

We decided it was time to start exploring and spent a very pleasant two hours sailing up the Black river with six companions, and saw water lizards four foot long, pure white Ibis, kingfishers, cormorants and a tree full of Flying Fox which is a fruit eating bat. Girls waded in the river up to

157

the boat trying to sell their flower garlands, their smiling faces quite beautiful. We went ashore at one point to visit a three hundred year old Buddhist temple, and a blind monk in his saffron robes was led to the door which he unlocked with two huge golden keys each about eight inches long. Inside there was the usual figure of Buddha who always appears to me to be very overpowering, but there was a lovely tranquil area much larger than the temple for meditation.

There was a policeman and his wife in our party from Bushey - Maurice and Sheila, who seemed to have adopted us and took us under their wing, fetching and carrying and making sure we had everything we wanted. It was nice to be cared for, and they booked beach beds for us in nice shady spots. There was one great drawback; one was pestered continually on the beach by local children begging. We went by taxi to visit some beautiful gardens outside Bentota, owned by a very distinguished man whose name I think, was Bevis or Bowan and who was Aide to the Govenor in the forty's before Independence. How we came to be there I have quite forgotten; we were the only ones from our party to go, however the owner gave us a very gracious welcome then handed us over to the head gardener who was very knowledgeable and knew all the latin names for all the plants. The gardens were a riot of colour and there were birds everywhere, we even heard a nightingale and one called, I think, a Dakar who could mimic a cat. There was a landscaped Japanese garden, a Chinese garden a series of pools and fountains and a variety of Bamboos, sculptures in appropiate corners and an Orchid garden. The owner sat on the verandah in an invalid chair and invited us to have tea with him, we enjoyed a most delightful morning.

There was a good beach here, though not suitable for snorkelling, but we enjoyed the swimming. We were due to tour the island in a few days time and were rather flattered when Maurice and Sheila asked if we would share a car with them, there were so many of their age group in the party they could have asked. There was a couple whom we named Tweeledum and Tweedledee, the latter a real extravert and very good company, we spent the evening with them and Maurice and Sheila but I had to retire early feeling very uncomfortable and was rather sick in the night, but slept all right later. I am afraid I was poor company for a couple of days and missed a few meals.

We drove into Colombo with two other couples and were allotted a lovely room in the Hotel Oberon, a very superior place, and I enjoyed a hot bath, but was still off food. We strolled into the city but all the big shops were closed and we were not impressed. After breakfast next day about twenty of us assembled and met our guide; a journalist named Alex and our driver named Mahi, and off we set sharing a car with Maurice and Sheila, and spent a rather tiring day visiting various ancient city sites: Anuradhapona, Ruvanveliseya, Dagobas all ancient Buddhist temples some about five hundred years bc. We arrived at the Village Hotel at Harabans for a two night stop-over. More ruins next day after a leisurely morning, this time at Polonnaraun, I am afraid I am not enamoured with ruins, although Alex certainly knew his subject and on telling us where our next visit was to be, he always ended by saying, "You WILL enjoy it."

En route to Kandy we paid a visit to Sigiriya Rock fortress which is a must for all visitors to Sri Lanka. This is a fantastic fortress built by a Prince for his safety and pleasure, on the top of a two hundred metre high rock and reached by steps carved in the rock face. We managed to climb two thirds of the way up to what was known as the lions Claw, and here there was a small platform where we rested and decided we did not fancy going any further. We took the descent quite gently; there were far too many people ascending and descending for our liking. We had a nice lunch at the Sigiriya rest house and I visited an extremely unpleasant toilet out of sheer necessity, stopped to see a cave temple – the last one we hoped – then paid an interesting visit to a Batik factory where we had the proceedure explained and saw the materials dipped in the various vats of dye, and on to Kandy where we were installed at the Topaz hotel, high above the town with a magnificent view.

Kandy is the second largest city and it is where Earl Mountbatten had his headquarters during the war. We visited the Botanical gardens where an ancient who had been a servant to Mountbatten escorted us round the gardens. We would have preferred to wander around on our own really, and we did not consider the gardens to be any better than those we had seen in Mahe. We called in at the market, all hustle, bustle, noise and smell as all markets are, but they have an attraction of their own.

We were taken to a gem factory where we were invited to purchase sapphires etc, then let loose on the town on our own until 5.50 p.m. when we met our guide who took us to the Temple of the Tooth to view the daily ceremony. This temple house, Buddha's tooth, is quite beautiful externally, but inside is full of garishly painted plaster. We had to join a queue and remove our shoes before entering to purchase a flower offering of Frangipani. I wish I had taken a photograph of Henry standing in the queue in his bare feet clutching his flowers, he remarked he "felt a right nit." We decided we could have omitted this bit of tourism, it certainly did not endear us to Buddhism. We were glad to retrieve our shoes and make our way back to the hotel where we invited our driver Mahi to have a drink with us. He is a very pleasant person of twenty six and already the father of eight. He was amazed to learn that Henry was seventy years old, his grandmother, he told us was bent and old at fifty, which is considered a great age.

We had a stupendous drive next day of about fifty miles to Nuware Eliya calling, en route, at a tea factory where we

160

saw the picking, drying, sorting and packing process, and given a cup of tea of course. Unfortunately my cup just fell off the handle which I was left holding, and the contents went all over the floor.

The drive itself was a series of hairpin bends climbing all the way to six thousand one hundred and eighty two feet, with magnificent views and great expanses of tea plantations with the pickers all busy throwing the tips into the baskets on their backs. Eliya itself is a bit dull, but still retains the air of the British Raj especially so at the Hill Club where Henry and I asked for tea after walking around the town. There were still old copies of The Tatler and Country Life on the tables in the lounge. This is were the British families came during the hot season and it must have been quite a place in those days, but the whole town had a faded tatty appearance, and gave one the impression that it needed a good clean up, although they did seem to be trying.

There was another magnificent run through the Ella Gap down to Wellawaya and lunch at Tissamaharama after which we went on a safari which was a complete waste of time. We were to have gone to the Game Reserve at Yala but it was closed to the public as the President of Singapore was there, so we had to put up with an animal sanctuary and saw absolutely nothing, and returned with sore backs and bottoms from the ride in the jolting jeep. Needless to say we were all a bit browned off and were driven to Tangalla which had a lovely beach but a ghastly hotel. The architect, we decided, must have gone mad. It was shaped like the prow of a huge liner, and we went down the hatch to cabin three on B deck, a really dreadful place. Henry's cousin Margaret Webb used to live nearby in a pleasant bungalow, her ex-husband was a tea planter, and I have the impression that she spent a rather unhappy time in Ceylon as it was then.

We were not sorry to leave this hotel, and en route for

Colombo we called at Galle which was a busy port before Colombo and has a distinct Dutch influence. We had lunch at Hikkaduwa, a wonderful centre for sea sports, where we viewed the coral gardens from a glass bottomed boat. Back in Colombo, and again at the Oberoi, we said goodbye to Mahi and were installed for the night.

Before leaving Sri Lanka I must mention that their temples mean a tremendous lot to the people: even when they have been reduced to rubble through age "once a temple always a temple" and the visitor is expected to treat them with due respect by removing shoes before entering and not posing for photographs in front of the holy monuments or paintings.

The airport was still chaotic but we managed to get through the proceedures showing our passports about six times, and wilting with the heat, Maurice, bless him, kept us supplied with cold drinks whilst we were queueing. Of all the airports we had been to, this was by far the worst.

THE MALDIVES

We boarded the plane and took off at 12.30 p.m. and having altered our watches by half an hour we arrived at Male at 1.20 p.m. It took us an hour to get through customs then we boarded a boat for the island of Baros together with six English and eight Swiss, and the voyage took one and a half hours. The first thing that registered with us was the beautiful clear sea, one would hardly need a snorkel. We were shown to our cabins, very primitive indeed with only the bare necesities and insufficient hanging space, we will still be living out of our suitcases, but what does it matter? All one needs here is a swimsuit, which we donned immediately and entered the dining room, which was a large round thatched area with open sides and plaited straw rolled up blinds which were let down for protection against rain.

Snorkelling

A word here about the Maldives, which consists of a chain of some two thousand islands of which only two hundred are inhabited, and were a British protectorate until their independence in 1965. The Maldivians had always been traders being strategically placed on the Indian Ocean routes, but fishing is now the main occupation. No place on the Maldives is more than two metres above sea level and no island has more than one hotel.

On the heavenly island of Baros we spent the time lazing in the sun, swimming before breakfast, snorkelling, sitting in deck chairs reading or watching dolphins playing around just off shore. The fish are exotic and I have never seen such a variety; different fish appear to inhabit particular coral and object to visitors swimming past. They come out on the attack in shoals – tiny black and white fish emerging from a forget-me-not blue coral; one can feel tiny pinpricks on legs and arms.

This is a tiny island; one can walk around it in fifteen minutes. On walking one day, we came upon a nudist colony of about a dozen, one of which was a London policeman who had been in our party all along, but always a loner and he was walking up and down the beach as though on his beat, one hand behind him and the other holding a paperback, a thriller I am sure! Our huts are only ten yards from the sea and we didn't have to bother with cash, just signed chits and settled up on departure.

We met the Hills who ran the Lobster Pot near Seaview on the Isle or Wight and had great fun snorkelling with them, but nothing could persuade Maurice to try the sport. It was not until later when we visited them at home and saw their wonderful underwater photographs, that we realised we could have hired an underwater camera on the island. So disappointing. It would have been lovely to have taken some for the record. This was a place of seclusion and complete relaxation, and after an idyllic week, which we enjoyed to the full, we left Baros, this time only taking forty five minutes to Male, and once again flew to the dreadful Colombo airport and took off three quarters of an hour hour late for London, stopping at Abu Dhabi for three hours whilst engineers repaired an oil leak in one of the engines. It was a most tedious night's flight and we were delighted when Ellinor met us and we learnt that all is well. So often on our return we are told of mishaps or illness during our absence. Such a welcome too from Benjy he is delighted we are back, and on arrival at Glebe House it was lovely to find the house warmed up and the Aga alight.

And so another lovely holiday came to an end. How fortunate we are to be able to go off like this and enjoy the warmth of the sun, to explore new places and see how other people live in different parts of the world. It takes some time to settle down again though, and it is all so cold.

RHINO SAFARI 1983

We were very uncertain about this trip and very nearly cancelled it as we were both feeling ill after a bout of influenza. Indeed, Henry was still on antibiotics but the doctor assured us that the sun would do us far more good than any of his prescriptions, so we checked in at Heathrow on February 26th and arrived at Nairobi at 8 a.m. local time. We were driven to the Panafric, which we know quite well now, and spent the day resting.

We left for Ambroseli Game Park in the company of a retired bank manager and his wife from Lancaster, who I only remember as Dorothy and Jim, and two young lawyers Gill and Graham Ashley from Burnley. He was a lawyer for Burnley Building Society and had visited Usk on business, and she was in private practice. We became good friends and, indeed they still correspond at Christmas time. It is nice to have some young company, in fact we are always attracted to the younger generation rather than our own. Hezeran, our driver, came from Mombasa and looked after us well during the whole trip.

Ambroseli possesses a wonderful background of Mount Kilimanjaro, which is Africa's highest mountain – some 5895 metres – and the peak is snow covered and used top be named "Kibo" but is now called "Uhuru" meaning Freedom, since Tanzania's independence. Only the foothills are in Kenya, the rest being in Tanzania, and it is an awe inspiring sight from anywhere in Ambroseli. From the lodge one could see forty or more elephant caked with whitish grey mud from their wallowing in the swamps, and then spraying clouds of dust over their backs. hippos do not appear white as they wash off their muddy coats. At the waterhole there were warthogs, which one is apt to dismiss as an ugly little brute, but seeing them in a family group grubbing around in the earth, trying to claim territory and hoping the larger animals would not notice them, they are so amusing, scuttering off with their tails erect like small flagpoles when frightened. We were told that they are quite dangerous, and would not hesitate to charge if in danger.

We had learnt the best time to see the game was early morning and after 4 p.m. as the animals rest in the shade in between these times, as of course, any sensible person should do too. We saw a tremendous variety of game before breakfast on our first day, and after a restful period went out again and found a family, a lioness with three very small cubs.

Hezeran thought she had only recently given birth to them in the bush. She was obviously leading them somewhere, and two of them kept up with her fairly well, but the third kept sitting down occasionally as though its legs were tired, and she, turning, would go back and give the cub a nudge, but eventually picked it up in her mouth and carried it. We watched and followed at a respectful distance, and eventually they reached a fine looking male asleep in the shade by a small pool. The adults nuzzled each other, then the male gave each cub a cuff and the lioness suckled all three. A truly domestic and touching scene.

I have heard people say that once you have been on safari you have seen them all, but we disagree. We have had so much enjoyment from watching the animals in their natural environment.

Next day we watched two young lions with a herd of wildebeest, one lay down on the perimeter of the herd and his companion kept charging in and worrying them. Hezeron told us they were probably waiting for three or more experienced hunters to join them, and this was so, but as nothing appeared to be happening, we moved on. We visited Tsavo west in the afternoon. Tsavo National Park is the largest in East Africa and is divided into east and western districts by the Mombasa – Nairobi highway, and the park is the home of some of the largest herds of elephant, often one hundred in number. Giraffes were numerous, looking down upon one with their disdainful stare, making one feel an intruder in their domain. Hezeron took us to Mzima springs where the pure underground water gushes out and supplies Mombasa and Malindi with drinking water.

On the far bank of the pools there was a concrete and glass underwater observation tank where one could watch the cumbersome hippos at their own level; they are surprisingly agile in the water. The birds were numerous in this area too and quite beautiful, rollers kingfishers, starling, weavers and waders of all kinds. The umbrella thorn trees seem to be full of black faced Vervet monkeys. Toothbrush bushes abound here; the natives use the twigs for scrubbing their teeth.

We arrived at Kilaguni lodge which is much nicer than Ambroseli and possess quite a large waterhole, and it was here that we watched a fascinating spectacle at first dusk. First of all quite a large herd of buffalo came to drink, then a herd of elephant – about a dozen – led by the matriarch who, trumpeting loudly, sent the buffalos to the far end of the waterhole. Gradually the elephants were joined by small groups of elephants appearing from all directions, the leader of these groups first approaching the matriarch, greeting her with trunks touching before quenching their thirst. The elephants numbered about one hundred we each tried to count sections. One is mystified as to how they communicate and arrange to meet. On leaving, each section leader approached the matriarch again as if to ask permission to leave before going on their way through the bush in different directions.

Gill, in our party is the expert photographer and is taking

photographs all the time. We were fortunate next day, to find two cheetah who had killed an Ostrich, taking it in turns to guard whilst the other ate, and were told they would be there all day eating and resting. Strangely enough there were no vultures around, which is normal at any kill, and no Jackal waiting for the leftovers. Graham had not felt well enough to be with us that morning, and as we were leaving for Tsavo East after lunch, Hezeran sought out the spot to show him the cheetah, and sure enough, they were still there. cheetah have been known to reach the age of fifteen years, and achieve a speed of one hundred km per hour.

We saw numerous Ostrich in this area; an amusing bird on the run looking so prim as if they were hurrying to catch a bus. At the lodge, the trumpeter hornbill was quite tame, coming down to share a sandwich at lunchtime. We are learning more about the birds, Hezeron's speciality, and now recognise the African Hoopoe, the Barbets, the honeyguide, which leads the natives to the wild bees nest, who, when they have taken the honey, will leave the wax for the bird.

We have added to our Swahili vocabulary too *Asanti* – thank you, *Chase* – tea, *Kahawa* – coffee, *Habani* – how are you? *Pola-pola* slowly and *Cweesha* – finish.

We spent a further week resting at our favourite place, Seafarers, on the coast, and then back home, wondering if we shall be able to do another Safari, we both hope so.

—————————— ೞഏ ——————————

BALI 1985

After a great deal of thought and discussion we decided to do what we grandly called our "World Tour", and spent two days at Kuoni's Head Office in Dorking, planning it all with their Specialised Tour Operator.

We set off from Raglan on Sunday January 20th, had lunch with Ellinor, and left Benjy with the family making a great fuss of him. We spent the night at The Copthorne Hotel, chiefly because in so doing, we could leave the car there for the duration of our trip. We were very impressed, the hotel being nicely appointed and the food good, and they drove us to Heathrow in a courtesy bus. Here we found the plane had been delayed by fog at Abu Dhabi so we had to spend a boring period waiting for boarding time, which was, eventually, 7 p.m. arriving at Abu Dhabi at dawn on Tuesday. The transit lounge here was quite fantastic, money no object of course, with marble floors and gold statues scattered about. On we went to Jakarta where we changed planes for Bali, were met and driven to Segara Village arriving at 11.30 p.m. and fell into bed without unpacking.

We met Paul next day, the Kuoni agent, who made sure we had everything we needed, then set out to explore our immediate surroundings. As the name implies, this was a collection of huts built as a traditional Balinese village. It had two swimming pools and a large straw thatched dining area. It was within walking distance of the modern Bali Beach Hotel which provided all banking facilities. The sea was lovely and warm, as one would expect, but we were disappointed to find it was not clear enough for snorkelling. The majority of the visitors were Australian, and very noisy

171

and brash they were too.

The island is roughly the size and shape of the Isle of Wight and we made arrangements to join a tour to see something of it, and to get the feel of it before exploring on our own. Our first call was a temple outside Denpasar, the capital, where we saw the Barong dance performed. This dance depicts the eternal fight between good and evil, Barong being a mythological animal representing good, and Rangda being the evil monster. Others taking part were a monkey, a Tiger, a Witch and beautiful Maidens, all fabulously dressed, and this occupied an hour. We watched woodcarvers at work, which particularly interested me, and were shown a family compound, which I felt did not give a true picture, as this was a wealthy family. On chatting to the drivers, who were all sitting around cross-legged, they told me of their family life. One said his family consisted of fifteen and they all lived together in one small house in a compound. We saw silversmiths at work, one of the main industries of the island, doing beautiful filigree work. The Balinese are a race of artists, painters, sculptors, dancers, actors and musicians. We passed the holy springs where all Balinese go to bathe, visited the elephant cave which was uncovered by archeologists in 1963, and thankfully returned to our village. The rattle of the bus, which was pretty ancient, the rough roads, our guide's continual dialogue interspersed by a noisy Yorkshire female passenger, and the heat, were all pretty devastating. Nevertheless, it was interesting to see the countryside, miles and miles of paddy fields, the farmers tilling the ground with oxen between the shafts, and continually meeting religious processions of worshippers bearing their offerings of shrines made of flowers and pennants on long poles, on their way to the temples. We were taken to a Balinese restaurant that evening to partake of a native meal – I imagined the meat to be tough ox – and were entertained by excellent dancers which included a troupe of small children – all very touristy.

172

The Balinese are deeply religious and they put daily offerings of exquisitely arranged flowers outside their doors. It was so sad to see them trampled on by uncaring and often inebriated tourists.

We hired a jeep and first visited Kuta, which was a mistake, it was full of Australian yobs, had a beautiful beach, only two interesting looking streets, a couple of nice looking hotels, but the rest was ramshackle lodging houses and junky shops. We left there in a hurry and made for the southernmost tip of the island, and here we found expensive looking hotels and houses standing in immaculate grounds, obviously catering for the well to do.

Back in Denpasar one gets the true atmosphere of Indonesia and has great difficulty manoeuvering around the swarms of trucks and motor bikes and the population walking the streets. The open shops display their carvings and materials, with brightly plumed fighting cocks in their cages.

Candi Dasar on the east coast is a delightful fishing port, with a few inns, shops, and eating houses. The small beach disappears at high tide, which is probably its saving grace, otherwise one imagines it would become like Kuta. Tulaben, further north, was busy with divers exploring a sunken U.S wartime vessel. We turned inland into the highlands, found the volcano area and walked over the solidified lava to the edge of one of three craters which last erupted in 1963, then on to Ubud, which has long been the centre for artists and craftspeople, and where one can absorb the Balinese culture. There was a weaving shed where we saw the most beautiful work being done for temple adornmment and ceremonial. On the way back to Segara, we watched flocks of ducks being herded through a village by men and boys with long bamboo poles, and there were chickens who retained their ability to fly, and apparently placid water buffalos being pushed around by small Balinese boys. I don't know if this is true, but we were told that the buffalo became quite wild if they smelled a European.

Bali must have been a lovely island in its unspoilt state, but as is the same everywhere, once there is an invasion of tourists a great deal of the charm disappears, which is sad. Tourism tends to cheapen the very thing that brought visitors in the first place. On the other hand, the beauty of the country should be shared as well as protected.

The owner of Sagara village entertained cadets and officers from a Swedish ship one evening, supplying a buffet, drinks and dancers, and advertising it as a wonderful place for a honeymoon.

We did one more trip inland to see the former royal temples, which was quite the best we had seen on the island. Set in spacious grounds with intricacies everywhere, and the royal cock pit – they did not put on a display, thank goodness! From there on to Sangel to see the monkeys, which, we had been told, could be seen in their thousands, they must have been terribly shy that day, we saw about fifty.

On the way back we encountered crowds of people everywhere, and learnt that it was a general holiday. We met and passed once again, numerous religious processions carrying a variety of offerings on their way to the temples

We were both ready to leave Bali finding it too touristy.

We received a telex from Kuonis saying that two cyclones had hit Fiji, but that crow's Nest, where we had elected to stay, was unaffected.

C3 80

AUSTRALIA

On Sunday February 3rd, a driver took us to the airport where we went through the usual tedious routine, and next day touched down on Australian soil about 11.30 and were delighted to be met by our old friends John and Jo Birrell, who drove us to Toorak. Both are so kind and gave us such a welcome, and on this visit they were determined to show us their farm which lies seventy miles north of Melbourne.

After a day or two at Toorak we packed both their cars, taking dogs and rations to their mini ranch. It consisted of about two hundred acres, and the small dwelling was originally a settler's bungalow, set in gentle undulating country where cockatoos, magpies, willie wagtails, crows and eagle abounded, and Kookuburras laughed away in the background, with snakes too!

They kept three bulls and about sixty head of cattle. The land looked very dry when we were there, but they had their own well which kept them supplied with clear water, and their own petrol pump, which was replenished once a month. They were considering retirement there, but I could not imagine them away from the city.

We stayed there three days, then returned to Toorak visiting old friends, then collected a car from Avis, and set off on Friday 15th, quite glad to be on our own again, although it had been great to see our friends.

The car was a Lasar and very easy to drive, but had no air conditioning, and we made for the Princes Highway putting up in a motel in Bainsdale where we enjoyed oysters and bream for our meal. We set off next day for the Snowy mountains and had a fantastic drive with spectacular scenery. It was a hard drive on a tortuous curving climbing road, much of it unsealed, before we reached Thrombo where we intended to stay for one night. The steep steps to all the available apartments rather put us off. It is a most attractive town with houses and chalets built in Swiss and Austrian style, and must be ideal for the skiing holidays for which it is renowned.

We drove on to Lake Jindabyne and selected a motel which turned out to be only mediocre. We had a more leisurely journey next day, staying the night at Eden on the coast, a delightful fishing resort, and on exploring, found the Fisherman's Club for an excellent fish meal. We decided to stay a second night and spent a pleasant day walking in the National park and climbing down to the beaches. Next stop for us was Ulla Ulla after a rather dull drive on a good road but through vast grassland and Eucalyptus forest, but keeping to the coast finding motels and enjoying excellent fish meals. We discovered one beach where Wallabys were quite tame, and came down to be fed by picnickers and campers. There were about forty of them looking rather scruffy we thought. Another beach that we discovered looked so inviting that, having it to ourselves, we stripped and had a bathe in the Tasman Sea.

We were to stay at Caryl's for a few days – Henry's niece – and found their house, not enjoying driving through the heavy city traffic. It was strange to see Marian, Henry's sister there, although we knew she was on a visit, which she had extended to see us – we usually see her at her home on the Isle of Wight. Here we became involved in the family, and it was lovely to see them all again, they came here about seven years ago. Neil had grown out of all recognition, he had become good looking and gifted too. Jayne had nearly completed her Physiotherapist course, and planned to use her qualification in the U.K after travelling abroad for a while, and Grahame had already left Australia, and had spent a little while with us at Glebe House, and was hoping to enter one of the services. Chris had a Professorship at Paramatta Hospital, but I think his heart was still at Barts in London. They had a nice house, a golden labrador named Sabre, a swimming pool and a cockatoo which came daily to be fed in the garden.

Grenville called and took Marian to the airport, but we heard later that she had been off loaded and was staying with Grenville, which did not please her at all. As a retired member of the staff of British Airways she was entitled to a free flight, but likely to be off loaded if the plane was full.

In the meantime Chris took a day off and drove us to the Blue Mountains, where we had a picnic, and took a ride on a scenic rail car high up in the mountains to view some super waterfalls, with colourful parakeets flying around.

We left Sydney on March 2nd, Caryl and Chris taking us to the airport, and calling at Grenville's to say goodbye to him and his little daughter Phillippa, and found Marian still there, but more hopeful of a flight on the morrow. We enjoyed our stay, Caryl and Chris had made us feel so much at home.

We found the plane quite restful after the hassle and noise of Sydney, and after a good flight, landed at Auckland.

NEW ZEALAND

We had both been looking forward to New Zealand, and, with hindsight, wished we had planned a longer visit. As the time was short we decided the only way to see as much as possible was to join a tour. We were collected by a minibus and set off in the company of two grass widows from Guernsey, a couple from Montreal, a French couple and two Japanese.

Our first stop was at Waitomo to visit some caves which seemed very ordinary at first, but with beautiful stalactite and stalagmite formations. Then we reached a cave, the ceiling of which was a mass of tiny lights – the glow-worm cave – and had to keep quite quiet otherwise the lights went out. At this point we boarded a boat on an underground lake and finally emerged into the sunlight.

We had lunch at a Kiwi farm, where we saw the culture of the fruit that has become so popular. In fact, the owner had relinquished dairy farming in favour of the fruit. He cooked steaks on a barbecue for us which was quite fun.

On to Rotorua, where, after a brief rest and a shower, we were taken to the International Hotel to attend a "Hangi" dinner and Maori entertainment. We were received by handsome Maoris who rubbed noses as a greeting, then led outside to see our dinner being taken from the hot springs where they had been cooked – great joints of beef, whole lamb and chickens had been wrapped and tied in canvas bags. We elected to have lamb, and how delicious it was! A huge Maori chief in his feathered cloak was master of ceremonies, and after the meal we were entertained by singers and dancers, a wonderful finale to a lovely day.

We toured Rotorua next day, visiting Whakarewarewa Thermal reserve which is entirely populated by Maoris and has a strange moonscape area with lava underfoot, and hot springs where people were doing their washing and cooking.

A number of houses had pipes extruding to allow the underground steam to escape – no worry about central heating bills here! The great Geyser erupted three times a day at irregular times, and we were lucky enough to witness this. The only warning one had was an underground rumbling, then a huge spout of water left the earth at boiling point, erupting to a great height, cooling immediately in the atmosphere and spraying everyone in the close vicinity with cool water. It was a most awe inspiring sight. There were holes in the ground with steam escaping, even on the golf course.

We were taken to the Agrodome, to see a show put on for the tourist, where we were shown different breeds of sheep with a running commentary and a demonstration of shearing given by an expert. The sheep dogs were a special cross of Collie and Labrador, exactly like our own dog Benjy in his younger days. These dogs travel over the backs of the sheep to reach the head of the flock to divert them. We called at Rainbow Trout Streams, a breeding centre which stocked all the lakes, and after lunch at The International and quite a long drive, we were delivered at our Auckland hotel.

As I remarked before, we wished we had had more time here, and would have liked to have visited south island too.

Our plane to Fiji was due to leave at 11.30 and after seeing our luggage loaded on board we saw it all being unloaded, and on being told the flight was delayed we were taken to a nearby hotel and given a room for the night. There was still no flight the next day, and we spent a very frustrating time, but took a bus downtown and walked around. Back at the airport we re-booked on the five o' clock plane, then changed to Air Pacific due to take off at 0020, and spent the time lounging in the airport. The delay, we were told, was due to a cyclone, which, unfortunately, means that we shall have less time in Fiji.

At last we boarded the plane, and a hostess decorated us all with a string of beads, which only made a furious Henry feel ridiculous as well, nevertheless, he wore them during the flight.

FIJI

The airport at Nadi presented a scene of complete chaos owing to the cyclones and the consequent floods. The homeless were everywhere, squatting on the floor together with their few belongings, and it was difficult to find room to plant ones feet, but eventually we made our way to the transport office. After a long wait and numerous phone calls, they managed to find a driver who was willing to try and get through to Crows Nest where we were booked to stay. There were many flooded areas and scenes of havoc, and at one point, our driver was dubious about getting through, but eventually we did, and were given a great welcome by the landlord, Paddy Doyle (no prize for guessing his nationality).

Crows Nest consisted of separate wooden bungalows, with a central dining area, and they did not appear to have suffered much damage. The telephone and electricity had been off for a while, and the staff had been unable to get in. We enjoyed a large cooked breakfast and spent the day sleeping and recovering from the ordeals of our travels.

The Fijians are quite delightful people, the men well built and handsome, their heads covered with a mop of frizzy hair, and usually their only garment would be the native sulu, a strip of plain cloth wrapped around the waist with the end tucked in, and it was not uncommon for the men as well as the girls to wear a hibiscus blossom in their hair. The girls were tall and beautiful. They are a mixture of Melanesians, Polynesians and Papuan peoples. Abel Tasman landed on the island of Viti Levu on 1643, then Captain Cooke in 1774, and Bligh in 1779. Great Britain took over Fiji in 1874 and the first resident Governor decided to keep the tribal system, which resulted in the Fijians owning 82% of their land, and tribal customs being kept very much alive. Half the population is Indian, coming originally as farm labourers, but today they are dominant in the commercial life.

The Fijians are very outgoing people and the visitor receives a warm welcome.

Mary Ola was the name of the girl who looked after us, and soon gave us the titles of *Tai Henry* (Grandpa), and *Bumba Carol* (Grandma) by which titles we were known for the rest of our stay, even seeing us on the other side of the street, she would hail us in this address at the top of her voice.

We went to Sigatoka, our nearest town, by bus to explore and to hire a car.

All the rivers had built up deltas, the channels of which were lined with mangrove forests, in fact there are some 50,000 acres of mangrove around the coast, and half the island's surface is covered with trees: sugar, copra and bananas being the main exports. In the town we came across a small steam locomotive drawing a long line of trucks loaded with sugar cane en route to the mill. Once or twice a week the same trucks pass by loaded with humanity who are given a free ride, this being the terms on which the concession to build a railway was granted.

The islands off Viti Levu have romantic names – Beachcomber, Treasure, Nana Castaway, Dick's Place and Plantation Village. The people live in grass huts with thatched roofs in the villages, but there were very fine houses in Singatoka and Suva, the capital.

We wanted to see something that was really Fijian, and on Sunday, we went to the Methodist church. The congregation was milling around outside, and immediately on seeing us, came over to shake our hands and welcome us. The people sang like angels.

We were privileged when Mary Ola invited us to visit her family mbure in a village about eight miles away, and here we were entertained and plied with their home brewed drink Kava, which is made from the powdered roots of the pepper family. The etiquette, we were told by Paddy Doyle, was to clap once before accepting a bowl, say the Fijian greeting "mbula", and down the rather bitter muddy juice in one gulp, then give two claps to show your appreciation.

There were two partitions in the mbure which were spotlessly clean, and the family of eight lived there. The roof looked as though it would be whipped off in no time during a cyclone, but we were told they pass a fibre made rope over the roof, through the windows, and anchor them at each end to the largest male members present. Nowadays they have advanced warning of cyclones, not so many years ago the huts would have been completely destroyed. The family slept on rush mats which were all neatly rolled up in one corner.

We visited the cultural centre Pacific Harbour, about 60 kms away, and which covers twelve thousand acres. We should have started earlier, the road was bad and it took us longer than we'd planned. We went aboard a double hulled canoe, which took a full complement of twenty, and were propelled by two large Fijians using bamboo poles round the island. At a promontory we were challenged by the chief, who sent his messenger on board, who then travelled with us acting as guide and explaining the custom and crafts of the people. At different landing stages we went ashore to see different crafts, i.e. rug and basket weaving, pottery, canoe building, implement making, cooking and tapa work. The latter was strips of bark stained and patterned with stencils. We saw different dances performed, and left rather reluctantly for the uncomfortable drive back. The lights went out during our meal that night, the electricity having suffered from the effects of the cyclones, and we retired by candlelight.

We had looked forward to doing some exploring on foot, but the weather turned nasty, so we drove to Singatoka and visited the temples and museum, and called in at the affluent looking hotel The Fijian, but found this to be far too sophisticated for our liking, and it was swarming with Japanese honeymooners. Agents apparently arrange the weddings and the honeymoon as a package. I cannot think of anything worse!

On returning to Crow's Nest we hired some sandshoes, which are obligatory for walking on the reef, and found this very exciting, I even found a bright BLUE starfish.

We changed the car next day as we were dissatisfied with the performance of the first one, and, taking a bite to eat and plenty to drink, we set off to visit Suva, the busy capitol. Here we saw the Parliament buildings, the Governor General's residence guarded by soldiers in white sulus, red tunics, and brass buttons, the South Pacific University, lovely botanical gardens, and a comprehensive and interesting museum. Turning inland we drove through flat dairy and beef country along the river, still very full, and on up into the mountains along a boulder-strewn track climbing a succession of hills.

The interior was beautiful and empty, with tree ferns overhanging the road and mongooses scuttling across our path. It was all so lush, with long soft grasses, many streams and luxuriant rain trees and the occasional self-sufficient homestead. We performed a taxi service for two giggling teachers who had missed the bus, dropping down to the fertile valley and passing through Indian communities with red pennants flying from poles in their gardens denoting that they were Hindus. We shopped for milk and bananas in case the weather improved sufficiently for us to sail to Castaway Island. Fiji is an archipelago of more than three hundred islands, one hundred and fifty of which are inhabited, the Castaway being the most popular to visit.

Unfortunately, it rained again next day and the sea was too rough for the passage, so we stayed in the hotel grounds, and strangely enough met a family who had emigrated from Wales. He had been a policeman in Pontypool, and she a nurse, and, stranger still, she was then working for Alan Mogg, the medical son of our great friend Dick Mogg from Cardiff, in New Zealand,

We explored the coast north of Sigatoka and found a lovely unspoilt and uninhabited beach; one wonders how long it would remain so for Fiji is developing fast as a tourist attraction. Henry managed to get the car stuck in the soft sand, but fortunately, with the assistance of a native, three small girls and four young men from a passing car, we were launched onto firmer ground. Swimming was not advised in the sea because of the presence of sharks, but we did have a quick dip here, it was all so inviting.

There is an annual festival called the *Balolo*. This is a sea worm which lives in the crevices of the coral reef, and which surfaces twice a year for breeding. The Fijians value them as tasty morsels, and work out exactly when they will rise, the date depending on the moon and the tide, and are there ready to scoop up the balolo in buckets and baskets, accompanied by a great deal of laughter and shouting. We witnessed a performance of the Meke, a dance performed by men and women dressed chiefly in leaves and flowers, arms and legs moving continuously and in unison accompanied by much clapping of hands and banging of wooden gongs. The men performed a separate wild war dance, their faces painted grotesquely, and brandishing clubs and spears. Then there were the famous firewalkers who came from the nearby island of Bega. In a large pit lined with stones, a pile of logs was set alight and allowed to burn until the stones were red hot, the unburnt wood was then removed, and the firewalkers dressed in a skirt of leaves, and walked in a circle on the stones with bare feet. It was reported that members of the B.M.A passing through en route for

Australia, carried out tests before and after the ceremony, but could give no explanation as to the immunity from injury. In fact, spectators were given the opportunity to examine the firewalker's feet when we were there. The Indians have a different firewalking ceremony which has religious significance.

Mary Ola taught us some Fijian – Hello is *Sa bula* pronounced Sahmboolah, Good-bye is *Sa moce* pronounced Sahmowthay, Thank you is *Vinaka*, Sir is *Turaga* and Madam is "*Mirama*, and we learnt that the hollowed-out log used as a drum with which we were called to our meals, was a *Lali*.

We were due to leave Fiji on Sunday March 17th, and on the Saturday a notice of a pending Cyclone appeared on the board, which was due by noon on Sunday, and Paddy told us during our evening meal that *Hira* as she had been named, was moving quicker than expected and consequently Nadi airport had been closed, so we resigned ourselves to a further stay at Crows Nest.

In preparation for the onslaught, Paddy handed us three candles, as the electricity always went off, black polythene bags to house our valuables, a polythene sheet to cover the bed and extra towels for mopping up, instructing us to close the shutters firmly. Being thus prepared we sat in our little chalet awaiting the unknown. The rain came in torrents before the wind started, and we had never known wind like it. The noise was tremendous and the roof was battered with coconuts and debris. I could not resist having a peep through the shutters to see the palm trees bending right over with their tips touching the ground, water cascading down the hillside, and rivers where the road had been. Needless to say we had no sleep that night and had a busy time mopping up. By 8 p.m. it appeared to have abated, and we cautiously opened our door with the idea of struggling to the dining area to see if there was anything to eat. To get there we had a major operation of clearing a path of piles of palm fronds and branches, but there was no-one visible, so we returned to our cabin and made ourselves a cup of tea with the last sachet (we had calor gas fortunately) and ate a stale cream cracker, and waited for the cabin to take off as the wind had found renewed energy. It appeared to ease off about 11.30 a.m. so Henry staggered out to reception, having to clear a path again as he went. We found Paddy who informed us the telephone wires were down, and there was no electricity, but he was going to try and take a car out to see if he could collect any of the staff, which, thankfully he did, and they provided us with an omelette, chips and a beer at 2 p.m. It cleared up about 4 p.m. but the airport was still closed, and the floods extensive, so we resigned ourselves to another unhappy night, but made the best of it in the company of other guests at the bar, and Paddy's yarns. The telephone was reconnected next morning, and eventually whilst we were having a sandwich lunch, we were told a car would be collecting us at 3 p.m. and a flight would be leaving for Honolulu.

The weather had been unkind to us, with only one day entirely free of rain and the delay of our arrival, thanks to cyclone *Govan* and of our departure thanks to *Hira* were unfortunate – but an experience. We loved the Fijians and their beautiful island, and were sorry we had been unable to visit others.

CS80

GRAND CANYON and SAN FRANCISCO 1985

We crossed the international date line and arrived Honolulu the day before, so we were still at Monday March 18th. Our hotel, the Pacific Beach, was a very splendid place, but I imagined all the hotels here would be. They had difficulty in finding our reservation, which was frustrating, as all we wanted was a pillow on which to lie our weary heads. Owing to the cyclones we had experienced in Fiji our time in Honolulu was curtailed, and on walking round next day and finding the famous Wakiki beach packed with Americans and Japanese, we were not sorry.

We had our breakfast in the Oceanic room, one side of which was filled by a huge tank reaching the height of two stories. During our meal a girl appeared in the water wearing flippers, a mask, an oxygen bottle, and wearing a very brief bikini, and fed the fishes from a bag on her waist. An American at the next table remarked in a loud voice "Gee, I hope the sharks don't get him," and when his companions pointed out that the swimmer was female, he said, "Oh yea, she got boobs!"

We put the alarm on for 6 a.m. for our flight to Los Angeles which is not a place we would choose to visit, but it was from here we had to fly to Las Vegas then on to the Grand Canyon. On arrival at the Amfac Hotel, a hotel for all passengers in transit, we telephoned to confirm our flight for the Grand Canyon, then found our way to the restaurant, and would you believe it – we had singing waiters!

On to Las Vegas next where we were taken to the Tropicana Hotel, a place which almost defies description. It was a mass of low powered electric lights of all colours, gambling machines all round the walls of a large lobby and betting tables down the centre playing roulette and pontoon, with queues of waiting gamblers. The impact of the noise and the crowded room was shattering and my idea of Hell. I swear the same people were still at the tables when we were searching for breakfast in the morning. We seemed to walk miles in the hotel looking for the pool by which we spent a quiet morning away from the brash and noisy scene.

A bus collected us at 1.45 p.m. to take us to the scenic airport where we boarded a plane, which had specially large windows for viewing, and we took off with about twelve other passengers. This, at last! was what we had come for.

It is hard to describe the fantastic scenes of grandeur over which we flew. Mountains and deep valleys in a variety of pinks, greens, reds and cream. This all started thirty five million years ago with an upheavel of the earth which created the Rocky Mountains. We followed the course of the great Colorado river, flew over lake Mead, the Hoover dam, and the Havasu falls. The bed of the Colorado has eroded to a depth of 1600 metres in places, and the erosion continues as the river, at a speed of nineteen kilometres an hour, cuts its way over three hundred rapids. We passed low over the Cataract Canyon, home of the Havasupai Indians, where some three hundred inhabitants live and cultivate two hundred acres.

Their village is only forty miles in a direct line from Grand Canyon village but two hundred miles by car. One can follow a trail by packhorse, which would be much more fun, and visitors are welcome. Visitors run the rapids in inflatables too, which I should imagine would be a hair-raising experience.

There were caves to be seen, occupied many years ago by Indians, and the spectacular Thunder river bursting from the rocks. From the air we could see numerous craters and trace the flow of lava down to the river, and as we flew over this wonderland of chasms and mountains of wierd and wonderful shapes, it seemed as though there was only just room for the plane to pass through. It was the colours that impressed us as much as the grandeur of the peaks and the depth of the ravines. One of the wonders of the world indeed and one we shall never forget.

After the flight, we were taken to the Rim to see the colours in the sunset, but oh! it was so cold, and a log fire at the hotel was a very welcome sight. Words are inadequate to describe the Canyon, and we were so grateful to have seen it, and after rising early to view it all again in the dawn, we left for the hell-hole of Las Vagos.

Saturday March 23rd, and we were not sorry to say goodbye to Los Angeles, and went on our way to see San Francisco. Henry had been there before and was eager for me to see it. We arrived at 12.30 p.m. and appreciated the fact that we did not have the hassle of customs etc.

A taxi took us to the Sheraton Palace where Kuoni had booked a room for us. It was a beautifully appointed hotel with a victorian elegance which we enjoyed very much after our spartan night on The Rim of the Grand Canyon. After booking a tour of the city for the next day, we went downtown on a trolley bus which is a MUST for the visitor, and yet another experience to add to our list. Being a Saturday, we had to join a queue and the bus was packed. We dismounted at the Wharf and joined the cosmopolitan crowd, with busters and vendors all trying to make a living. I had the impression of an exciting and vital place. It was cold, and rather than queue again for a trolley, we took a taxi back to the hotel, and enjoyed a hot bath and a delicious meal in Lottie's bar. After breakfast in our room on Sunday we were collected for the city tour. We had an excellent courier/driver and saw one house which had withstood the earthquake of 1906. We were particularly interested, as

Henry's father, an architect, had seriously considered coming here to help with the rebuilding, but the advent of Henry rather changed the idea.

It was difficult to imagine the devastation of that time, most of the buildings being of wood and disappeared in horrendous fires, and the beautiful Sheraton where we were staying suffered; the marble pillars toppled, but like the rest of the city, rose again on the same site, and one can read the list of names of august guests in the lobby: emperors, kings, presidents, authors, actors and actresses. The tour over, we were dropped off at Fisherman's Wharf, a tremendously exiting place with a wonderful selection of fish restaurants. We chose Chicks where we had Clam Chowder and beer, everywhere was crowded and noisy.

Later we took a boat from Bay Town and sailed round the harbour. The sun was kind but the wind was cold, but we enjoyed it all immensely, especially the colourful crowd. Whilst waiting in the queue for a trolley bus, we were entertained by a demonstration of kite flying, the like of which I had never seen before.

We were leaving for Los Angeles again the next day and did not know how to spend our spare day so we asked the Bell Boy's advice and he gave us three options - a trip round Hollywood to see the homes of famous stars; a tour of the city or a trip to Disneyland. None of these really appealed but we rashly chose the latter. A bus collected passengers from various hotels en route and went through the turnstiles with about five hundred other people. Henry was immediately accosted by a jovial coloured lady saying, "congratulations, you are a winner," and pinning a badge on his chest saying just that. On asking what he had won and why he was told "free entrance for another whole day" which was not much good to us, so we pinned in onto a small boy behind us, who was delighted. Our entrance covered everything apart from food and drink, and we were quite bewildered by it all.

We decided to travel on the Monorail first of all to get our bearings, and from then on it was non-stop. We had a ride on a horse drawn wagon, a people's car and a paddle steamer which took us round an island passing various scenes on the banks, such as a Settler's hut set alight by marauding Indians, and realistic Moose drinking at the water's edge.

We were disappointed that the queue for the Yellow Submarine was too long to join. A family parade took place at three in the afternoon celebrating thirty years of Disneyland, in which all the characters took part. It was a wonderful world of fantasy for children and grown-ups alike, and we were surprised at how much we enjoyed it.

Our wonderful trip at an end, we boarded the plane for Gatwick on Wednesday March 27th. On recovering the car and loading up, we started for home only to find the brakes had frozen and we had to contact a garage to sort us out. Henry, from then on always left the car in gear.

What a wonderful trip it has been, seeing old friends and new sights which we will recall with much pleasure, and we appreciate how fortunate we are to have been able to do it all.

— CႽ␠ —

TANZANIA 1986

We went here in February hoping to view some part of the great migration of the wildebeest. This is the month we always favour to leave the U.K but the best time to see the wildebeest trek is in July and when the rains are over in September.

We left Raglan on St. Valentine's day, drove to Smith's Cottage and made arrangements with Ellinor who was away skiing with all the family, to collect the key from a neighbour and take her dog Barty together with Benjy to the local kennels for a week, after which they would collect both dogs.

It was so slippery and icy up the lane to the kennels that we left the car and walked the dogs up. Benjy expressed his disgust, but Barty could not care less so long as he is fed and has Benjy for company. We drove to Heathrow and stayed a night at the Penta, where we were able to leave the car for the duration of our stay, and after spending a leisurely morning went in the courtesy bus to the airport and eventually boarded a KLM for Amsterdam.

Here we had to change planes and had a dreary flight to Vienna where we were joined by a party of obvious climbers making for Kilamanjara. At Khartoum we had to wait for No.2 engine to be checked, and eventually arrived at Arusha 09.30 Sunday February 16th. What a journey!

We were tranferred to our hotel The Meru Mount, which was very scruffy, and lacked the amenities of toilet paper, a plug for the handbasin and a bedside light that worked, but this was the general impression one has of this poor country

197

which is struggling so hard to make ends meet.

We met the rest of the party, twenty one in all, and had a meal of Goulash which I found inedible, and wondered if it was wildebeest. During the meal our baggage was broken into in the bedroom. We had left our cases unlocked, which was unusual for us, and nothing had been stolen, but the cases had obviously been turned over. Several people had this experience, and one couple had had a lot stolen. To me this is understandable, the people are so poor, and in their eyes the tourist has everything to be desired. We retired early and after a good night's sleep and a breakfast which was more acceptable than the previous meal, and consisted of paw paw, small green remarkably sweet bananas, toast and butter. Unfortunately, the coffee ran out, then the supply of cups, and we were reduced to collecting cups from people who had finished; washing them ourselves, then queuing up for whatever was left – a very disorganised meal.

We then had to sort out our luggage, taking the absolute minimum on the trek, and packing the remainder into a locked case to be left in a locked room, and after the experience of having cases broken into, one just hoped for the best.

We shared the safari bus with a couple from Surrey and another from Hayling Island who were good company, and as usual we were the oldies, and met our Tanzanian driver named Kea. We drove along a fairly good tarmac road for about forty miles, then a further forty on a very rough road to Mama Gibbs. This was originally a coffee planter's estate, with a beautiful bungalow standing on a rise overlooking the plantation and surrounded by lovely gardens The government had taken over the land but had allowed Mama Gibbs as she was known, to remain in the bungalow and run it as a guest house. Here we had a very good lunch, chiefly vegetarian. The gardens were a delight, and we could have spent a lot more time there watching the delightful weaver birds building their nests on the tall reeds in the pool.

We had an even worse drive after lunch, the state of the roads are appalling, and full of potholes, and this is the general state throughout the country.

We suffered a puncture, which was not at all surprising, and eventually arrived at the Ngorongoro Wildlife Lodge, a beautifully situated building built on the edge of the crater. This crater is a caldera – the remains of a crater that has blown its top covers one hundred and two square miles, being nine miles across, and is some 2,500 feet deep, one of the biggest craters in the world, and the actual conservation area is 2,500 square miles.

Looking down from the Lodge the view was spectacular, with a large lake immediately below, and one could see the movement of animals with the naked eye, clearly through binoculars, and very well indeed through the fixed telescope.

There was no electricity or water at the lodge when we arrived, both came on at 6 p.m. – a daily routine – and we were able to enjoy a shower before our meal, which we hoped, would be better than the previous night's. There was a heavy thunderstorm soon after our arrival, but the clouds lifted, and we fervently hoped it would be fine for our visit to the crater on the morrow. We got up at 06.30 and after breakfasting we left for the crater, keeping to same company, but this time travelling in a very decrepit Land Rover.

Entry to the crater is by an extremely steep and winding track down the slopes of the crater wall, known as the Lerai descent which is negotiable only by four wheel drive vehicles. This took us an hour, the driver having to manoeuvre round huge boulders as one had to hang on for dear life. The crater bottom is mainly open grassy plains with some fresh water lakes, swamps, and two dense acacia woodlands, known as the Lerai and Laindi forests. The animals and birds are abundant and the list too long to record here. We took another track out of the crater, which seemed worse then the descent, passing one broken down Land Rover with its passengers sitting on the edge in a very disconsolate manner, and we were very relieved to get back in one piece.

We had lunch and were ready to go off again in our original bus with our driver Kea, bound for the Serengetti. This is the largest and best known of Tanzania's National Parks, and covers approximately 5, 600 square miles. It is a vast open plain with lofty rocky outcrops, acacia woodland, savannah and scrub with rivers, swamps and the occasional small lake.

The migration, as I have said, takes place in June or July, sometimes earlier, and consists chiefly of zebra and wildebeest moving from the central plains and into a corridor travelling westwards, six to ten abreast in a winding column several miles long, seeking fresher pastures in the rainy areas before they travel south again back to Serengetti.

We were extremely fortunate to see them in their thousands, one minute grazing placidly, then suddenly lifting their heads, sniffing the air then starting to run in two's and three's to join the column.

They were visible as far as the eye could see, a great mass that formed into a moving corridor. The zebras were first, as they crop the longer grass followed by the wildebeest with the carnivores on the outskirts who are ready and watchful for the weaklings and stragglers as easy prey. The Mara is famous for the black-maned lion which lounge about in the sun seemingly docile and oblivious to this mass exodus. Many wilderbeest drop their young on this trail, to be guarded by two or three companions whilst she licks and nudges the young who must be on its legs immediately to stumble along until it is strong enough to run with the mass.

We went to investigate when we saw a number of vultures in trees, and found that a mother had given birth and she was unable to get the calf on its feet. The vultures watched, waiting for it to die. I longed to get out to see if we could assist the animal, but Kea said no, there must be something the matter with it and it would not live.

Later, looking down from an escarpment, we saw a stationary Land Rover and thought we also saw a cheetah. A figure emerged from the vehicle and waved to us, and we thought we were being invited to see the cheetah, but no! we were frantically waved away. Two girls from the wardens lodge had tranquillised the animal and were waiting for the drug to take so that they could put a collar on it which contained a transmitter to enable them to follow its movements.

Here the lion is often found resting in trees, the male possessing a magnificent black mane, and as we drove back to the lodge we saw the majestic figure of one looking down upon us from a rocky height. We saw animals and birds in abundance and arrived absolutely filthy and worn out and very glad to find a beer, have a cold shower and some food which is generally poor in Tanzania.

I was awakened about 2 a.m. by the roaring of a lion which sounded alarmingly close, but on peering out into the darkness could not see anything, and despite the interruption awoke feeling fresh in the morning. After a poor breakfast of a small banana, some mango and dix bread, and having to queue yet again for a cup and having tea because the coffee had run out, we met up with our party for a more leisurely drive into the game park. We were warned by fellow travellers to keep the latch on the sliding glass door in our room, as the baboons were apt to enter and empty the cases searching for goodies.

On this trip we came upon several hippos in a murky looking pool, two males fighting, with massive jaws wide open, for the possession of a female, and the conqueror then starting to mate, which act Kea informed us went on for twenty minutes and the female only came up for air once, with all the others looking on and refereeing. Kea was delighted to be able to show us a lion and three cubs in a tree, a lioness in another, and again three lioness in a tree with a lion standing guard on the ground. We saw two magnificent cheetah which Kea and another driver started to follow unmercifully, until we pleaded with Kea to leave the poor creatures alone. There were zebra and wildebeest amassed that day as far as the eye could see with three lioness stalking the latter and we left them to their hunting. We had hoped to have a further drive after lunch, but a terrific thunderstorm broke so we were confined to the lodge and were without water all day the trouble being that everyone uses it as soon as it comes on at 6.30pm. After a good night's sleep despite the animal noises in the background, chiefly zebra and lion, and the usual scramble for breakfast, we set off for the long drive to Lake Manyara National Park, stopping at Mama Gibbs again for lunch. This is a small park covering one hundred and twenty three square miles and is noted for its birdlife. At times the lake is visited by thousands of Lesser flamingos, but we were not fortunate enough to see them. We stayed at the Lake Manyara Hotel which is perched on an escarpment overlooking the Rift Valley. The park is lush being fed by several small rivers and there are forests of mahogany trees, giant fig and acacia woodland. We were unable to identify all the birds we saw, and Kea was no ornithologist, but we did see herons, the honeyguide, hornbills and Ibis and the colourful starling and Widowbird. We were glad to have a plentiful supply of water at last, and were able to wash the dust from our hair. We shared a table with Shirley and George Barr from Jersey and discovered that she originally came from Handsworth in Birmingham and that her father, a builder, actually built the house in which my Uncle Hubert had lived.

We visited the Olduvai Gorge where we saw a display of bones and fossils uncovered by Louis and Mary Leakey, it was they who discovered the bones of a creature 1.8 million years old in the Gorge, which was the oldest find until Richard Leakey in 1972 found a shattered cranium simply lying on the surface in the fossil beds, apparently washed out by recent heavy falls of rain. Following Leakey's studies we had a picture of these men who stood under five feet tall, had low foreheads, bulging eyebrows and brains about the same size as a gorilla. Hundreds of stone axes and cutting tools had been found in the same area, and it is reckoned that there are still many secrets locked up in Lake Turkana.

The Ides of March arrived, Sam's birthday, and after a very disturbed night poor Henry had been bitten by mosquitoes on his eyelid and lips and looked a horrible sight. We had breakfast, packed and left for Mount Meru, where we collected our cases from the stores all of which were safe and sound, thank goodness! Kea drove us to the border where we said our farewells and changed buses for Ambroseli.

Back in Kenya we felt we had arrived back in civilisation. Tanzania is so poor and one has the impression that there is a real struggle to keep going. We arrived at Ambroseli Lodge, our second visit here, with our tongues hanging out and appreciated a bath and a meal.

I was unable to join the safari next morning as I succumbed to the tummy bug, and after an awful night during which I thoroughly disgraced myself, spent the morning in bed dosing myself with Diocalm. Henry however saw a cheetah with a cub, a herd of about forty elephants and two Saddlebill storks. I was furious with myself but felt quite incapable of doing anything. I joined the foursome next day and enjoyed seeing plenty of my favourite elephant, eight lioness with two cubs and rhino. The driver proudly pointed to five wildebeest, but having seen literally thousands, we were not impressed. Ambroseli is a real dust bowl, one gets covered in dust and eats it too, and we were all coughing, it was a good idea to have a covering over the nose and mouth. After lunch we left for Nairobi and as my tummy was still troubling me, was glad to arrive at the Panafric. It was nice to know ones way about, but I did not enjoy the meal very much, although it looked much more appetising than the meals presented to us in Tanzania. It was a joy too to have a nice bedroom with plenty of hot water and everything in working order, and we began to feel and look quite human again. We spent a lovely lazy day. After enjoying a good breakfast we walked into the city, did some shopping, had a leisurely coffee at The Thorn Tree watching the world go by, changed into swim suits on our return to the Panafric and spent the afternoon in and out of the pool, not socialising at all. We met up with our travelling companions for a farewell drink before dinner.

The Serengeti and Ngorongoro visit has been a wonderful experience, albeit a bit primitive, but we are so glad to have done it, and we went off to the Jardini Beach north of Mombasa for a week's relaxation. Jardini was a much larger complex than we were used to, and there was nothing to write about as we spent the time in a repetitive manner, swimming, eating drinking and walking. We went along the beach to have a toasted sandwich at the Nomad and met Julie there. It was her parents who ran Ocean Sports at Malindi, of which we were very fond, but we learnt that they had sold it and retired to Kilifi. We met one interesting character at Jardini, who popped out of her room as I was passing on my way for a swim. She was from Manchester and she and her late husband, both Jews, had escaped from Germany, leaving behind all their possessions. After taking many menial jobs they set up in their own business in the rag trade. She was nearly ninety and went for a swim before breakfast every morning, taking a skipping rope with her, which I never saw her use.

The north coast of Mombasa did not appeal to us as much as the south of which we were very fond, but we thought a change would be good, and we did not know what we were missing. We again hired a car and went to visit Seafarers, and were delighted to find the original owners back in charge, the government having taken it over for seven years and the contract now ended. Ocean Sports too, as I have said, had changed hands. Somehow I think this will be our last visit.

And so, after a week's rest, we caught our plane from Nairobi to Heathrow, and arrived on March 12th, and quite relieved to find our car still parked at the Penta, where we spent the night, and had a happy reunion with Ellinor and her family before driving back to Raglan.

CAIRO and the NILE 1987

We arrived in Cairo on Sunday February 1st at 21.00 hours and after a 45 minute bus drive arrived at the Mena House Hotel feeling very hungry, thirsty and tired. We had an omelette in the restaurant and fell into bed. We were up at 7.45 a.m. next morning to enable us to have breakfast before assembling with others for a bus to take us into the heart of the city. Driving through the city one has the impression of crowded streets, chaotic traffic, blaring horns, and struggling pedestrians in a haze of dust. On emerging from the bus one is assailed by the smell of spices and decaying rubbish, and kites circling around overhead.

Guess where?

The Citadel is the most prominent landmark and is

surrounded by enormous walls and battlements built by Saladin during the time of the Crusades, when he successfully defended Cairo. Inside the Citadel is the most spectacular building, the Mohammed Ali Mosque. Of all the places we visited that morning, to me the most interesting was the Museum, where one could spend days not just the two hours we had. Our guide, a petite girl named Hela, was a most knowledgeable Egyptologist and spoke excellent English. We spent most of the two hours in the Tutankhamen section which was magnificent and quite incredible. The boy king died at the age of about eighteen and really it is the modern discovery of his tomb virtually intact that has made him the most famous of the Pharaohs. It was wonderful to be able to see all the treasures that were buried with him in his tomb, articles that supposedly he could not do without in the life hereafter. He was embalmed and placed in a series of gold coffins one inside the other, and residing eventually in a golden sarcophagus. His tomb, which we were to visit later, was discovered by Howard Carter in 1922, a small tomb compared with those of the Pharaohs discovered earlier and which had all suffered from robbers pillaging them, but this one was found to be intact, being built beneath the larger tomb of Ramases.

The view of Cairo from the Citadel is quite remarkable. One can see the old city and the new, minarets galore pointing to the blue sky, and the Nile weaving through the crowded city, a haze of dust hanging over it all, and miles away to the west, the Pyramids and a vast expanse of desert.

We shared a taxi with two fellow travellers and returned to the hotel. Most of our party were going to see old Cairo after lunch, but we decided we had done enough for our first day, and after quenching our thirst with a welcome cold lager and a light lunch we lay in a horizontal position by the pool.

The most notable excursion from Cairo is, of course, to

the ancient Pyramids of Giza, a distance of only eight miles. The Pyramids are visible almost as soon as one leaves the city, and suddenly one enters a desert plateau after passing through an intensely cultivated area. I have the statistics of the great Pyramid where the Pharaoh Cheops was buried, but these I think, are boring, but will say that the base is a perfect square and the actual building of the edifice is mind boggling with only human resources available. It is assumed by archaeologists that the tomb was robbed of its treasures as the burial chamber contained nothing but an empty sarcophagus but some people believe that the ancients were more cunning than at first thought, and the Cheops and his treasures still rest in some chamber undiscovered. One can ascend into the interior through an entrance 55 feet above ground, which is far from easy, being steep, airless and, I found, very claustrophobic, but there was a Bedouin here and there to give a helping hand en route to climbing the succession of passages leading to the Great Hall and beyond to the King's chambers. I did not find this at all rewarding, and on emerging an Arab approached me indicating that my blouse had come undone!

The building of the Pyramids apparently depended on the seasons of the Nile, the peasants being barred from their agricultural activities at certain times of the year and forced to work on the building, which entailed first, the building of a road to transport the stone, and this took ten years and a further twenty years to build the edifice. There are three smaller Pyramids built in honour of members of the royal family, and, of course, the Sphinx, which was excavated from the limestone and looked very much the worse for wear, being badly eroded. Before we left the area, I had my first ride on a camel which was quite and experience. From there we were driven to Sakara to view the most ancient Pyramid, and to go underground into a great corridor where, ranged against the wall, standing eleven feet high, were gigantic sarcophagi containing relics of the Bulls of

Apis – the sacred Bulls.

On our return we went aboard the *Neptune* for our sail up the Nile, and made ourselves familiar with the craft, which was well fitted out and the cabins roomy and comfortable. M.S *Neptune* was started in 1977, took four years to build and made her maiden voyage from Cairo to Aswan in 1981.

Modern life goes on along the narrow cultivated strip on either bank, where intensive agriculture is carried on, and one sees many villages and the primitive processes of cultivation and irrigation worked by the fallahin – the peasants. Tremendous expense must have gone into the building of the palaces, mosques temples and pyramids, yet one still sees the ass working a water wheel, and villages built of mud. The cliffs are dun coloured, the only trees to be seen are the date palms, and the waters of the Nile looked pretty filthy, with the occasional carcass floating by.

We went ashore on two or three occasions to visit a temple, but the highlight was Denderah, where we called at the Valley of the Kings where the Pharaohs constructed their tombs which were excavated from the rocky walls of the valley and this is where we viewed the tomb of Tutankhamun, the only one to avoid robbers. More than sixty royal tombs lie in the valley. Karnak Temple, a short distance across the river, is the largest and best preserved in Egypt, and indeed, the world, being dedicated to the sun god Amon-Ra and dates back to 1900 BC. It has massive pillared halls with every surface covered in hieroglyphics recording the deeds of kings and gods. We visited Luxor, Thebes, Esna to see the Barrage and Temple, Edfu with the two thousand year old Temple of Horus, Komombo which has a Temple of the crocodile god Sebekh, and on to Aswan.

The first dam at Aswan was built in 1902, but as the population grew, more water was needed, and the larger dam was built, and the water built up by the dam formed a great lake-Lake Nasser, which stretches for three hundred miles south with an average width of six miles. The building of this dam began in 1960 but as the dam grew in height, so the water rose in the lake and threatened two magnificent temples those of Abu Simbel which were carved out of the mountain and were discovered at the beginning of the 19th century. To save these temples Egypt approached the United Nations Organisation, and urged their members to help save them, which they did, and after several plans had been rejected, it was decided to cut the temples into large blocks and assemble them in a higher position, and this work began in 1964.

There were engineers, architects, archaeologists and workmen from different nations all living together, first in tents and huts on the banks of the river, and as the waters rose, houses were built on higher ground, and a small town was formed, with shops, offices, a club, a cinema and swimming pool.

The moving of the statues was a tremendous achievement. To reach the roof of the temples the top of the mountain had to be removed, and during this operation, to prevent damage to the statues, they were protected by a great pile of sand, and eventually the cutting began. This must have been a most precarious task, cutting into sandstone three thousand years old, and the statues were cut into one thousand and forty two blocks with not a single block cracked or broken. The cutting was completed, and in January 1966 work started on the rebuilding of the temples on the new site, and at the end of the year they were complete.

Domes with an artificial mountain covering them were built as a background for the temples, and the work which began in 1964 was completed in 1968. It was a great experience to climb the modern staircase and enter the dome which formed the mountain backdrop to the statues.

Excursions on the Nile have become tremendously popular. Thomas Cook was the first to offer cruises in steel constructed steam powered cruisers and sailing dahabiyas, luxuriously fitted out and fully staffed, towards the end of the 19th century, and early in 1900 they had built several fast two hundred and thirty foot paddle steamers which sailed the Nile from November to April. At the peak of the popularity of Nile cruising between 1900 and 1915, some thirty ships were operating at the same time, but at the outcome of the first world war through to the end of World War II, cruising died, and it was not until 1977 that new ships began replacing the old. There is now a boom, Nile cruising is the highlight of any holiday in Egypt, and one still sees one or two of the remaining 1900 paddle steamers.

Back in Cairo, we explored the busy souks and bazaars. It is interesting to note that Egypt is where pigeons were first domesticated and formed into breeds, and the training of carrier and racing pigeons, and indeed, raising them for eating is an Egyptian passion that goes back hundreds of years. At times the markets are full of barely-fledged pigeons, live ducks and chickens in crates between carts piled with onions, garlic, lemons, artichokes broad beans and tomatoes. There is a special pigeon market - the souk el hamam near the Citadel, where boys and old men gather on a Friday to sell and exchange birds.

There are boat trips on many rivers in the world, and although we have experienced no other trip, one reads of sensational scenery and beautiful cities on their banks, but the Nile offers something quite unique in mystery and antiquity.

---------------------------- ∞ ----------------------------

THE GAMBIA 1988

We had been many times to the west coast of Africa, but knew nothing of the east coast and decided to explore a little of it in February 1988.

Relaxing

Gambia is a tiny state extending some two hundred and

fifty miles from the coast in the centre of Senegal, and is little more than the banks either side of the curling river Gambia, the country being about thirty miles wide at the mouth of the river, narrowing to fifteen miles at its eastern border. It became politically independent in 1965 after a long period of British colonial rule. Banjul is the capital and it dates its beginning to March 1816 when a Captain Grant arrived with seventy five men from the fort of Goree near Dakar, who were looking for a suitable site from which to control traffic on the river, and negotiated with the king of Kombo to take over Banjul island, a low lying sandy spit, which he named Bathurst after the then colonial secretary in London, and the town had a spectacular growth, with civil government beginning in 1818. It became politically independent in 1965. Tourism began here in 1976 and by 1984 over thirty thousand visited the country and these figures rose to seventy thousand in 1986 bringing a tremendous revenue and employment with many hotels being built on the Atlantic coast.

We stayed at the Atlantic hotel just outside Banjul which was half an hours drive from the Yumdum (a lovely name!) International Airport. The hotel itself was disappointing to us, not our scene at all, being far too big with about two hundred bedrooms, entirely self contained with swimming pool, boutiques etc. but very little beach. We were told it was not advisable to bathe in the sea and not safe to go outside the hotel grounds unaccompanied. We, being used to exploring on our own, found this entirely alien and when we wished to go into the town or elsewhere, the doorman would whistle a taxi or provide an escort.

The great attraction is the wild life on the river, and ornithologists come to watch and photograph over five hundred different species. The Abuko Nature Reserve is the smallest reserve in the world and is a short taxi drive from Banjul which we visited with two young friends, (both doctors from Birmingham) whom we met in the hotel. This was a fascinating jungle in the middle of the savannah. There is a large notice at the entrance reading, "PLEASE remember you are a guest in the home of these plants and animals, so take away only memories and photographs and leave behind only footprints."

Here there is a successfully functioning Ape rehabilitation centre. Chimps and Gorillas born in captivity in Europe and America are taught how to live and survive in natural surroundings, and once they are qualified to adapt themselves to nature they are set free on Baboon Island up river near Georgetown. There is an Animal Orphanage and an Education Centre adjacent to the crocodile pool, where we saw ten crocodiles basking on the banks.

One follows the track on foot, and how much one sees depends on how observant one is, as the fauna are very well camouflaged, and one is very conscious of many eyes watching from the tall trees and on the ground.

As the jungle is surrounded by savannah, it provides a perfect habitat for a great variety of birds. Amongst many we saw the beautiful pigmy and the giant kingfisher, and were very fortunate to see a black heron walking through the shallows forming a tent with its wings to enable it to catch small fish in its own shade. Some visitors reported witnessing a life and death struggle between an African python and a crocodile. The battle apparently lasted about ten minutes, the crocodile being the victor.

One can take a ferry from Banjul to Barra and about six miles to the east is a village famous for its sacred crocodiles where people go to take part in the ritual bath which us purported to be a cure for barren women and stomach ailments. Juffureh, about twenty miles south and just inland from the port of Albreda, is the ancestral home of Alex Hayley, author of *Roots* the story of the Kinteh family, who, I understand, still live in the compound.

Albreda itself became a French trading post in 1681 and together with the British Fort built on James Island in the middle of the river, played a big part in trading in the Gambia region. Later, when under English rule Albreda was a destination for many slaves who could claim freedom upon reaching the flagpole in the village square.

I regret that Henry was not at all well during our visit, sadly it proved to be the last holiday we had together, and we were not able to explore as much as we would have wished. A happy outcome of this holiday is that we made firm friends with Fiona and David Ratliffe, he, at that time being a consultant at the Queen Elizabeth hospital in Birmingham, and Fiona in general practice in Selly Oak.

The Gambians expect a greeting before any conversation even if it is only a small question. In the local language the greeting is *Salaamalekum* but an English "Hello" will do, and the natives seem to spend a great amount of time exchanging greetings before getting down to the business in hand, and they shake hands as often as they see each other, on meeting and on parting.

Their dress is bright and colourful and should cover the whole body, the men wearing khaftans or warambas - long gowns with elongated armholes worn over baggy trousers, and the women wear long dresses, many with elaborate head-dresses to match. They are tall and stately people. Wearing trousers is considered inappropriate, as they tend to show the line of the thigh, whereas bare breasts are not considered immoral. However, the tendency of tourists to walk around Banjul in shorts and bikinis scandalises the elders who fear their younger generation may imitate them.

The National Women's Bureau issued a brief counsel about the appearance of tourists in The Gambia reading thus "The staff of the Women's Bureau would like to express its concern about the effects of the tourists season on citizens and residents of The Gambia. While walking in the Banjul area, it is apparent that the tourist is unaware of our local dress standards. Scantily dressed men and women walking in public places can be a great embarrassment to the Gambians. Perhaps if the tourists were made aware of cultural and religious customs, they would not mind wearing more discreet clothing away from the confines of the hotel." This, I feel applies to many countries we have visited, and one should respect the customs of the host country.

We returned home to a sad time, Henry's health deteriorating, ending in his death in October. Thus ended a very happy fifty one years together, the last twenty of these since his retirement, have been very eventful, and we have been fortunate in being able to visit so many countries and see so many wonderful sights and cultural traditions of many races.

CBℇO